Comments from Our Rea

"If you've ever shared your home with a cat, you will relate to every bit of this book. Beautifully written! Adorable photos. What a cutie pie! And my black cat, Merlin, has a crush on her!"

Cheryl B. – Author, Producer

"Destiny is a very special cat, like the one I had and loved some years ago. If he and Destiny are in touch with one another, I wonder if Destiny could teach mine to channel. I'd love to know what he was thinking when he tried to climb my Christmas tree."

Phyllis H. – Author, - Palm Desert

"Highly readable, whimsical, humorous, and interesting to hear about the world through a cat's eyes and sensibilities."

Richard A. – Publisher, Los Angeles

"I just read your book and it's so special. Very clever and sweet. Anyone who is a pet owner or a parent can relate…Thank you for sharing this amazing book with me."

Judy S.R. - Producer, New York City

"As you know, I ADORE cats. I read your book in one sitting. Such a delicious read! I even read portions of the book aloud to my hubby and showed him the photos. Keep me in mind for the follow-up book." **Terza W. – Los Angeles**

"Loved it! It really flowed. Destiny was a delight to know when she was living on Sutton Place, when we were all young. Reading her story brings back happy and sad memories but I loved reliving Destiny and Fern's lives at the time. I think you have a winner!"

Nina D. – Santa Monica

"What a sweet read. Cat lovers, animal lovers, just about anyone would love experiencing Destiny's story. I can't wait to hear what happens to Destiny next stage."

Michelly F. – Hollywood

"The book reads like a smile; the sound of a fun time, with children and adults all dancing together."

Peter A. - Hollywood

"Destiny is very special. What a sweetheart!"

Lynne M. – Hollywood

"Wow! Destiny is incredible! I read it in two evenings and was absolutely enthralled. This book is one in a million!"

Laurel D. - Miami

"No one can remain unmoved as Destiny and Fern find each other and begin to build a life together filled with heartfelt love and insight into each other's needs."

Jeanene S. - Palm Desert

...and from our Furry, Feline Friends:

"I live with John and Alex on Sutton Place. How come we never go to the Hamptons?!"

Luigi

"I wish my life was as interesting as Destiny's."

Merlin

"Living on Sutton Place sounds more interesting than our place here in Santa Monica. And summers in the Hamptons sounds fabulous, doesn't it, Gracie"

Lucky

"Destiny's story has made some great bedtime listening. Can't wait to hear more."

Clendenin

"What happened to Destiny's mom was so sad. I'm glad Destiny found Fern and had a great life."

Isabeau

Thanks to all of you who read our prototype and gave us your input and comments.

For those of you who are reading this now – please like us on Facebook: Theycallmedestiny, follow us on Twitter: @destinykalser and send your reviews to theycallmedestiny@gmail.com.

Your friend,

Destiny 🐾❤

The DESTINY Books

THEY CALL ME DESTINY

The story of the first year of my life.
Spans February to September 1963

DESTINY'S CHILDREN

The story of my one and only litter – 7 kittens to be exact.
Each one with a different personality! We found homes for
5 and 2 stayed with us.
Spans October 1963 to Summer 1972.

DESTINY MOVES TO LALA LAND

The story of our move from New York City to Los Angeles
Spans Summer 1972 to Summer 1977.

They Call Me
Destiny
a Meowmoir

From a gutter in the Bronx to a fancy condo
in Manhattan and weekends in the Hamptons

Destiny Kalser
with Fern Field Brooks

Books 2 Cherish
2554 Lincoln Blvd, #619, Venice, Ca. 90291.
(310) 823–2460   Books2cherish@gmail.com

ISBN: 978-0-9912583-0-7

Library of Congress Control Number: 2014922830

Book design and layout by Debra McCormick
McCormickDesignLA.com

Photos by Konstantin Kalser

Visit our websites:
books2cherish.com
Theycallmedestiny.com
Like us on Facebook (Theycallmedestiny)
Follow us on Twitter (@Destinykalser)

Printed and bound in the USA by RR Donnelley

Dedicated to

CINZIA MANGANO
who loved me without knowing me –

LOIS DE LA HABA (my LOLO)
who encouraged me to finish this book –

and... to cat lovers of all ages who will relate to many of my
experiences and hopefully will take me into their hearts.

Your friend,

Destiny 🐾♥

P.S. Thanks also to:

Debra McCormick for her support and dedication as well
as the cover design and book layout –

Paul Chepikian for the enhancement and tender loving
care of my very old photos –

And especially to **Geri Jewell** who coined the word we all
now love – MEOWMOIR!!!

Acknowledgements:

A special thanks goes to all our galley readers: authors, editors, publishers, agents, colleagues, friends, family, cat lovers,(and cats) for your time, your support, your accolades and your notes.

A special thanks to Lois, Geri, Cheryl, Thom, Christie, Judy, Philip, Jeanene, Phyllis, Linda, Michelly, Andy, Aileen, Donna, Chris, Richard, MaryLou, Nina, Lynne, Terza, Joel, Laurel, Peter, John, Debra and Paul.

Thanks also to Luigi, Merlin, Lucky, Gracie, Clendenin, and Isabeau.

And of course, to Cory, Konny, Marcie. Without you, this book would not exist and our lives would have been far less interesting and happy. We love you all.

Fern and Destiny

Table of Contents

PART ONE
The Beginning of My Journey

I | Prologue

They call me Destiny. Funny name, isn't it? What? Oh no! I didn't say I *was* destiny. Magari! (That's an Italian expression that my owner, Fern, couldn't translate, even though she majored in languages at Columbia University and even teaches Italian to this day! Anyway – "magari" means something like: I wish it were true!) Let me explain.

I first wrote... or rather first *told* my story in Italian. It all started when Fern sent a picture of me to her mother in Milan, Italy. And then her mother showed it to a friend and her little daughter, Cinzia, who was 8 years old at the time. Well, apparently Cinzia fell in love with me – or rather my picture, I guess.

When Fern told me that – I was really touched. A little girl – half way around the world – loved me and she had never even met me. And I kept wondering what Cinzia was like. So one day, on the way to Montauk in the car, I started talking to Cinzia in my head – you know, pretending she was right there, sitting next to me in the car. I started telling her the story of the first year of my life and that's how this book got started.

And I had to do it in Italian because that's the only language Cinzia could understand. But then Fern translated my story into English – so now I can share it with you my friends, fans, and readers, and I'm thrilled.

Anyway – as I was saying, I'm not "destiny". I'm a black cat. Cinzia already knew that because she had seen my picture. And you know it because that very same picture is on the cover of this book!

So, as I talked to Cinzia in my head, I began to explain to her that they call me Destiny because that's what my owners named me. Although, to tell the truth, they hardly ever called me that, but you could say it was my "official" name because it's the first name I ever had. After a while though, my owner, Konny Kalser, (Fern's "significant other" at the time, I guess you would say), nicknamed me "Espresso" – like that little cup of strong Italian black coffee – because I'm all black and, for one reason or another, I kept him up all night – just like an "espresso".

Then one day, out of the blue, and without even warning me, they started talking to me in German because Konny was born in Germany, and I became "Katzchen", which in German means "little cat".

When Fern talked to me, she almost always called me "Katzchen", except for those times when she just said "scema" (pronounced like "shore" – that's Italian for "idiot") or just "Aho!" in the Roman dialect, accompanied by the appropriate gesture of her hand. (This – the gesture with the word said in the right tone of voice – and with the right look – means: "Hey stupid! What are you doing now?!") But, don't get me wrong – there was nothing hurtful in those words when Fern said them to me. I could tell by the tone of her voice and the look in her eyes that she loved me.

So I soon knew English, German and the Roman dialect quite well, but not much Italian because they hardly ever talked to me in pure Italian. So, it wasn't easy for me to tell my story in that language – especially to a little eight-year-old girl – but I decided to try anyway. You know – if someone falls in love with you just from a photograph – it's the least you can do. It wasn't easy though. And now, I'm expanding my story so you can visualize the world I lived in then and, since hindsight is always 20/20 – to help you better understand everything that was going on in my young life at the time, and in the lives of the people who loved me enough to take me in.

So – to finish with the name business – "Destiny" in English, isn't masculine or feminine the way "il destino" is in Italian. Apparently, most of the masculine words end in "o" and feminine words end in "a". Go figure!

I know all this because in those days Fern taught Italian and did some of her tutoring in our home and I listened in. In English we don't have masculine and feminine endings so "Destiny" can be a name for a girl or a boy cat. That worked well for me, and for my new "parents" as well, because in those days they didn't have a clue which gender I was.

And, they gave me an English name because I'm American. That is, I was born in America and have

4

lived here all my life, so far anyway. One of my parents, however, might have been Siamese or Burmese. At least that's what I've heard people say when they looked at me and Fern often liked to speculate that I was part Burmese. She really liked the way they looked and these days there's even a whole breed called "Bombay" like the city or the gin. Fern researched it and it seems in Britain they crossed Burmese with black domestic cats, while in America a lady in Louisville created the breed by crossing *sable* Burmese with American *Shorthairs*.

I have no idea what the difference might be but anyway as I said and just between us, when my owners named me they didn't know enough about cats to even figure out my gender (I'm a girl cat), much less recognize my Asian heritage, so a vague name like "Destiny" suited me to a "T".

You, my friends, have a name from the very first day you're born if not sooner. But I had to go around for three months just like that: anonymous, unknown and unnamed. As if I didn't even exist! Finally though, my real life began. It happened like this.

II | In The Warehouse

I was born in the dead of winter. I know it was winter because it was very cold and snowing and if it hadn't been for the warmth of my mother's body and that of my brother and sister, born just minutes before me, I don't know how I, or any of us, could have survived even for a day.

At first my siblings and I weren't hungry because my mother seemed to have plenty of milk. As I look back on those days I guess that her long absences when we were very little meant she was out foraging for food. We didn't understand that so the first time we woke up shivering because she wasn't there, we thought we would never see her again.

Actually, we couldn't really see yet so we huddled close to each other and whimpered so softly it would have been a miracle if anyone had been able to hear us. But our mother kept coming back. And soon we learned to just keep each other warm and wait for her return.

After a few weeks though, once our eyes were able to see, she started to nudge us out of the nest she had made in a hidden corner of what I now imagine must have been a very big room. At least it seemed pretty big to us. I'm not sure where we were but now that I'm much better travelled, I'd say we must have been in a warehouse or supermarket storeroom of some kind. All I know is – there was little activity at night but in the daytime there were lots of feet scurrying around, with boxes being picked up and dropped all around us so we never ventured very far out of our corner. Which was a good thing because one day I almost got squashed by a box dropping not more than an inch from where I stood shaking. Naturally my mother scolded all of us and reminded us once again that we must never be seen and always to keep out of sight of the people around us.

One day however, just as the last workers were leaving, my mother got caught trying to sneak back in. They picked her up and threw her out the back door, telling her never to come in here again. The door slammed shut, the lights went out and we were left alone in the darkened surroundings. Scared to death, we huddled together and despite all her warnings for us to keep quiet we started meowing at the top of our lungs hoping to get our mother to understand she needed to come back. That night we fell asleep, cold and hungry — and alone!

III | On The Move

The next morning we awoke, still cold and scared – and hungry. We wanted to call out to our mother but there was already a lot of activity all around our hiding place and we knew better than to make any noise at all.

Some time later – we had no way of knowing how much time had gone by – we began to think we better get out of that place if we didn't want to starve in there – when suddenly our mother was back. I guess she had waited till almost all the people were gone and then quickly sneaked back in before anyone saw her. Or so she thought. Suddenly, boxes were knocked out of the way and our secret hiding place wasn't so secret anymore.

A lady dressed in a dark coat, hat and gloves was peering down at us as our mother hissed as fiercely as she could manage to scare the lady away.

"So this is why you were so eager to sneak in," the lady said, trying to make friends with our mother. "I bet your little ones are hungry – and you need to feed them. Let's see what we can get you." She disappeared and our mother heaved a sigh of relief as she licked each one of us, teaching us how to always be well-groomed, even under the most awful circumstances.

Soon the lady was back with some milk and food for us and although she smiled and talked softly to us, our mother wouldn't let her get anywhere near us so she soon stopped trying. She turned around, put back the boxes to shelter our hiding place, turned off the lights and went away.

Our mother must have been very hungry because she ate and drank everything the lady had put down and then she stretched out and soon my brother and sister and I were full of her warm mother's milk and then we were sound asleep.

The next day our mother nudged us awake very early and sort of pushed us out of our hiding place. At first we couldn't figure out what was going on but soon we realized she was getting us ready to move because now that we had been discovered she figured we better find another place.

We didn't know exactly what she had in mind, and frankly, I don't think she did either, but while she was trying to figure it out, my brother and I decided to play. Our bellies were full and we had had a nice sleep so we were having a grand time chasing each other, and tumbling and rolling over each other and my mother encouraged my sister to join us because she knew there was no better way to strengthen our young legs. We had the best time that morning running all over the place until our mother heard the key in the door and called us back into our hiding place.

That night the nice lady brought some more food for us but it seemed both she and my mother knew this would not be a good place for us forever.

The next day my mother was gone for a very long time again. She came back just as it started to get dark and the place was quieting down as it always did before they finally closed the door. She told my brother and sister not to make a sound, picked me up and quietly headed out into the night.

Very soon I felt (more than saw because my eyes were shut tight as she carried me by the scruff of my neck) my mother jump onto what seemed to be a ledge, and then she slithered under something I later learned was a slightly open window and we dropped down onto a very cold, hard floor in a very dark, damp place.

She put me into a corner where she had obviously created a make-shift home for us by using a wooden crate, and some old newspapers and then she disappeared. I was very cold, and alone, but I tried very hard not to be scared.

Somehow I instinctively knew my mother had gone back for my brother and sister so you can imagine my surprise when she returned a little while later without them.

She was really upset so I didn't ask any questions but I could tell how unhappy she was and she must have gone out a hundred times during that night to circle the place where we had been living, looking, and calling out to my brother and sister without a second thought about who might hear her. We weren't that far away from our original place so I could hear her but no matter how loudly she called, there was no answer.

The next day she went out almost before daylight but apparently she couldn't get into the old supermarket storeroom which I now know was our old hiding place.

Later on I realized – and she must have too – that it must have been Sunday – because we remembered there was always one long period of time when there was no activity in the storeroom and I and my siblings could roam around and play whenever and wherever we felt like it.

The next morning she again ventured out really early, but again she came back empty–handed and now she was more upset than ever. She made several more trips – apparently sneaking into the building in the daytime and circling it at night to call out to my siblings – to no avail.

Finally, after a few days, she confided to me that maybe the nice lady might have taken them because it might have looked like we had gone away and left them behind. In any case, she explained to me that we needed to keep looking for a better place to stay because it was much colder and darker in this new place and there was no way we could survive there. So, after looking for a few more days for her other kittens, my mother sadly led me away from that place where I was born. I had no way of knowing I would never see it, or my siblings, again.

IV | A Terrible Accident

So began our regular, new, routine. We usually hid in the daytime and travelled by night so no one would see us. That was especially easy for me since my fur was all pitch black. For my mother it was a little more difficult because she was black and white, but we managed to survive and even found some food almost every day.

I was amazed at the tasty snacks that humans throw away. As we sifted through garbage (because by now I was getting bigger and could help a little) we found many scraps of good things to eat and I realized my siblings and I could have eaten very well almost every day just on the things that people throw away. That thought made me very sad and I had to admit I missed my brother and sister more each passing day. There was no one to play with and my mother seemed to be getting sadder and sadder. And it was sort of lonely with just the two of us. We never saw any other cats, or even people, on our nightly searches for a better place to stay.

And then the winter got harsher. It started to snow almost every day and sometimes the snow was like little balls of ice (I know now you call that "hail"), and it really hurt if we couldn't quickly find a place to hide from the wind, snow and hail.

So, it wasn't easy. Sometimes my mother would hide me away in a corner somewhere and go looking for a new place for us to sleep. At those times I think she would also return to the warehouse to see if maybe my brother and sister were there. She never said anything to me about them but I knew she was very sad.

At other times we went out together because I was getting stronger every day and that way she didn't have to double-back to bring me to our new hiding place. We must have slept in a dozen old buildings during that time and each one was worse than the one we had slept in before.

It was on one such night that she was carrying me because I got too tired to go on my own. It had started to snow again and we were surrounded by a lot of noise – which I now realize were cars and horns blasting away. Suddenly I heard my mother utter a terrible howl and I was flying through the air. I landed with a thud and hit my face hard on the ground and then everything went black.

When I opened my eyes again I could hear my mother's heavy breathing not far from where I was so I pulled myself in that direction and curled up next to her. She shuttered, gave my face a loving lick and then she went still.

PART TWO
From The Gutter To Sutton Place

V | Being Rescued

I guess I must have fallen asleep because when I opened my eyes it was daylight. A cold, gray day with the wind howling in my ears. My mother was next to me but I was surprised she provided no warmth and seemed to be very stiff. As I slowly started to become aware of more of my surroundings and circumstances, I realized there were voices talking softly very close to my ears. It didn't sound like the people we used to hear in the old building. And soon I realized it was two little girls looking down at me.

Girl 1 – "I think it's opening its eyes."

Girl 2 – "There's some dry blood around its mouth."

Girl 1 – "The mother is dead."

Girl 2: – "I know. Let's take them to your house. We can take care of them there."

Girl 1 – "OK. Get the kitten. I'll take the mother cat. We can bury her in the backyard. We can't leave her here."

One of the little girls picked me up very gently and wrapped me in her arms and put me under her warm coat. The other little girl carried my mother very carefully and I could see a lot of love and sadness in her eyes. I knew exactly how she felt.

When we got to their back yard there was a lot of whispering and planning. They wiped my mouth with a warm, wet cloth, brought me some milk – which wasn't nearly as good as my mother's milk had been – but I wasn't about to refuse any act of kindness.

I wasn't sure what they were doing but after bringing me the milk they seemed to be putting together a kind of bed in a big box. This box was different than the kind of boxes that surrounded us in our first home. Those were mostly soft and light and I later found out they were made of cardboard. This box was hard and on one side there was some kind of see-through material like I had seen surrounding some of the places my mother and I passed during our search for a new home. It was strange because you could see through it but you could not get through it to go where you thought some food might be. Only sometimes we got lucky because we would find a small opening and we could squeeze through that fencing but those times were few and far between.

Finally, after putting me gently onto the old blanket that was to serve as my bed, they lowered the side of the box with the see-through material, hooked it up, and then took my mother and went away.

VI | The Chicken Coop

It got very quiet after they left and I started to look around at my new surroundings. There wasn't much to see so I headed toward the side of the big box – which I later learned was an abandoned chicken coop – to get a closer look at the see-through material. Of course, I again tried to get out, but although there was some give in this wire mesh, it was securely held in place. No holes or openings that I could squeeze through. However, I could see out a little into what turned out to be one of the little girl's (Marcie was her name) backyard.

It was quiet in that backyard and seemed to be a safe place for me but it was also very, very cold. And when the wind blew, there was nowhere for me to hide except under the blanket which didn't help much. Luckily on that first day in the chicken coop the sun finally came out so that the sunshine, together with the blanket, gave me a little bit of warmth. But it wasn't going to be enough. I somehow knew that without my mother and my siblings to keep me warm, I was going to freeze to death.

I rested for a little while and then continued to take my tour around the chicken coop. The little girls had locked the part of the wire mesh that swung open so I already knew that did not give me a way to escape. The rest of that see-through wall was very sturdy and there were no broken links or places anywhere where I could squeeze through the way my mother and I had done several times in our travels through the back alleys of the area. There also was a solid floor instead of the soft earth we usually found under fences so there was no chance I could dig my way free. As kind and caring as the little girls were, I was trapped in a place that was going to be the death of me.

I took another look around, curled up under the blanket, and resigned myself to my fate.

VII | Will I Survive?

I guess I must have fallen asleep because the next thing I knew I was being picked up, cuddled and petted. Marcie, one of the little girls, was holding me close to her chest. Her body heat was wonderful and my trembling from the cold was beginning to subside.

The next thing I knew she was smearing some warm milk on my mouth to encourage me to eat. I think she even put what I now know is an egg in with the milk because it tasted different from the cold milk they had given me the night before. The sun was coming up and Marcie whispered to me that it was going to be a warmer day and I began to think maybe I might not die in this big box after all.

Life went on like that for a few more days. Marcie came to see me as often as she could I supposed, and sometimes she brought me some things to eat. But sometimes she didn't bring me anything at all. And I really didn't understand why she didn't take me with her when she disappeared into the house. I could see it clearly from the chicken coop, and sometimes an older lady came out to do some chores around the backyard. I knew enough to stay very still and quiet when she was nearby but she seemed like a kind person and I really didn't think she'd mind if Marcie took me into the house. I started to wonder and plot how I could make that happen because what I knew for certain was that I could not survive for very long where Marcie was keeping me.

However, I also had no idea how I was going to get out of this mess I was in or what I would do if I did get out. Where would I go? What would I do? I was little and alone. So all I could do was settle down in the chicken coop and hope that it wasn't going to rain or worse yet – snow.

You people have a saying that humans plan and God laughs. I had no way of knowing that my life was about to dramatically change. I knew Marcie was desperately trying to figure out a way to keep me safe. I had heard her tell the other little girl (who had not been around for the last few days) "My Grandma will never let me have another cat." I thought this was strange because I hadn't seen any other cats (although I very much would have liked that!) – so I really didn't know what she was talking about.

As we sat there that morning, Marcie started to tell me a little bit about herself. She explained that since her mother had died recently, her best friend, Cory, visited as often as she could.

"She loves you too," explained Marcie, "but she also has other animals, and I don't know how long I'll be able to hide you here and I don't always have enough money to buy you something to eat…" As her voice drifted off her eyes welled up with tears. "Cory's coming back to visit today. Maybe we'll figure out a way…"

She hugged me closer to her chest as the tears streamed down her face. We looked at each other sadly and really there was nothing left to say. Neither she, nor I, could imagine that there would ever be "a way!" There was no solution to our dilemma.

What neither one of us could know was how dramatically circumstances (or fate, or destiny, if you will) were lining up to change my life in a magnificent way. From the stories I've heard – it went something like this.

VIII | My New Home

One day my future owners were going to the Bronx to pick up two little girls and take them to the movies in the city. Coincidentally, these little girls were eight years old too – just like Cinzia. Cory, short for Corinne, was my future owner's daughter, and the other one was her best friend, Marcie.

As fate, or "destiny" would have it, I already knew these little girls because they had been my saviors.

As I told you, shortly after we had to move out of the warehouse where I was born, my mother and I became the victims of a hit-and-run driver. My mother must have died almost instantly, but luckily Marcie and Cory found me the next morning lying in the gutter with blood running out of my mouth. They took me home, but Marcie was afraid her grandmother wouldn't let her keep me – because they already had a cat, a dog, and a bird, so she hid me in the empty chicken coop in their back yard. Marcie had also recently lost her mother – so you can understand how and why we bonded so quickly. We spent several afternoons just being sad together.

Anyway, Marcie and Cory – when she came to visit on weekends – were really very kind to me. Whenever Marcie's grandmother gave them money for candy or ice cream, they would put it away until there was enough to buy me something to eat. It wasn't easy though. Whole days passed when they couldn't buy me anything at all. And, even though they came to talk to me quite often, it was very lonely. I missed my mother and my sister and brother terribly. And it was dark in that chicken coop and unbearably cold. After all, it was mid-February in the Bronx, so the day they forgot to latch the chicken coop, I went out.

Well, with my luck (or should I say "destiny"?) – just as I stepped out of the coop and tried to get my bearings, I heard a terrible noise. I whirled around and froze in my tracks. There was an enormous brown mountain tumbling towards me, making a terrible racket. Of course, I immediately started running in the opposite direction as fast as my paws would take me, but the mountain kept following me with incredible and frightening speed.

It was Marcie's poodle and now I know that he didn't really want to hurt me. He only wanted to play. But at that moment I can assure you, my friends, I was scared stiff.

The poodle caught up with me at the back door of the house and sat down, blocking my way. So, I sat down too, and started meowing at the top of my lungs. Luckily, Marcie, who has keener ears than a mouse, heard me. This is what happened.

IX | How I Got My Name

Marcie and Cory were sitting in the back seat of Konny's car with Fern – my future foster mother – sitting up front in the passenger seat. They were waiting for Cory's father to come out of the house where he was talking to Marcie's grandmother so they could all go to the movies in the "city" – which I later found out is what New Yorkers call Manhattan.

Suddenly Marcie heard my voice (I'll never know how – over the noise of the dog barking) and eyes wide with terror, she whispered to Cory:

"I hear a kitten meowing!"

Cory, her eyes wide with fright as well, added in a whisper: "It got out!"

Fern, sitting in the front seat, couldn't help but overhear this whispered conversation between the two little girls sitting in the back seat.

"But how could it get out if you closed the latch?" Marcie asked.

Cory replied: "What do you mean if _I_ closed the latch. _You_ closed it."

Marcie countered very severely: "Cory! You were the last one there!"

Cory, now totally petrified, could only manage a feeble "Uh oooooooooh!"

At this point Fern, who had followed their exchange very carefully, asked: "What is it? Do you have a kitten? Do you think it's loose? Should we go see?"

"Oh yes!" shouted the little girls as they jumped out of the car and ran towards the back of the house, with Fern bringing up the rear.

They all barreled down the steps which led to the back yard and saw a big, brown "mountain" (which was Marcie's poodle) looking down at a tiny black hill (which was me).

He was sitting there just looking down at me and blocking my escape. And I was sitting there, absolutely terrified I might add, just looking up at him, trying to figure out how I could get away.

Suddenly, there was Cory running towards me. She scooped me up and brought me to where Marcie and Fern were standing.

Now by coincidence, or luck, or "destiny", or whatever you want to call it – Konny (Cory's father) had told Fern that he wanted to buy her a kitten because she had said she liked them. But she tried to dissuade him for a variety of reasons.

First of all because she felt having an animal was too great a responsibility. Their life wasn't suited to it. They traveled a lot; kept irregular hours; were always surrounded by lots of people, and so on.

And secondly, because according to her, there are two things you just don't "buy" – perfume and kittens!

You see, ever since Fern was a little girl, her father often went to Europe, where in those days perfume cost a lot less than in America. So when her father returned from his trips abroad, he always brought back bottles and bottles of perfume – for Fern, for her mother, for everybody. Fern was little then and probably didn't realize her father wasn't finding the perfume on the street. He had to "buy" it somewhere. But – never having seen him do it – she never gave it a second thought. Even after she grew up – she somehow always expected perfume would be there.

And then, any time in her life she had ever wished for a kitten, someone had given her one as a gift. Once even a Persian kitten of great value. So, according to Fern, you just don't buy perfume or kittens.

But, since the thought of having a kitten had already entered her mind (even though quite negatively for the time being) when Marcie said to her: "Would you take it home? Oh please, please take it home with you." Fern thought for a minute and then answered: "Yes. All right. We'll take it. It must be destiny."

So, that's how I got my name, my personality, and when my real life began. But just then, Konny, Cory's father, appeared. He looked at me for a long second and then asked: "What's that?"

Honestly – men! As if he'd never seen a cat before?!

So, my owner (she was no longer my "future" anything because she had already adopted me in her heart) answered: "It's our kitten."

"Oh," said Konny, while I held my breath. Then, after what writers call "a pregnant pause", as if he had just heard Fern, he added: "What do you mean 'our' kitten?"

I thought I was going to faint as Fern explained: "Well, Marcie found it and was keeping it in the chicken coop in the backyard, but since she can't keep it, she asked me if we would take it and I said yes."

Cory and Marcie were just standing there wide–eyed, and probably holding their breath, just like me. And I have to tell you that Konny didn't exactly jump for joy when he heard of this new addition to his family. Planning to buy a kitten is really quite different from having one already on your hands – or worse yet – underfoot. Especially since he was really quite obsessive/compulsive about having everything in its place. But he accepted me; Fern and the girls smiled and I heaved an even bigger sigh of relief.

Later that evening I heard Fern whispering to Cory that I was lucky Konny wasn't like her father had been. Apparently Fern's father had been *very* superstitious and would never have allowed a totally black cat in the house or anywhere near him. In fact, she said, if a cat – of any color – ever crossed his path he would turn around and walk the other way. And he never would have sat down for dinner at a table with exactly thirteen guests. Ironically, Fern had said, he passed away on a February 13th. So, a black cat, in his house? Never!

Wow! I thought to myself. That was really a close call. Fern's right. Her dad would never have let her take me in.

Luckily (although I learned later that Fern paid attention to a lot of strange things) – she didn't share this superstition with her father. In fact – she was fascinated by everything "occult". She was even taking a course in "witchcraft" at the New School in lower Manhattan. She thought she'd be learning about witchcraft itself but it turned out the class was actually about the *"history"* of witchcraft. Naturally she was disappointed but decided to stick it out anyway and ended up enjoying the class.

So for the moment the fact that I was a pitch black cat was not a problem and the five of us headed out of the backyard toward the street. I took one last look at the chicken coop that had sheltered me for the last few days and wondered what life – or "destiny" – had in store for me next.

X | Too Good To Be True

It took me a few minutes to recover from my frightening encounter with Marcie's poodle, and then the one with Konny, but after a few minutes in Fern's lap, I was composed enough to look around and make a quick inspection of what turned out to be the family car.

It was blue, with leather seats and a wood-paneled dashboard. There was a radio and even a telephone! Some of you may be reading this in the 21st Century where cell phones are nothing unusual – but this story takes place in the early 1960s and trust me – a mobile phone in the car was a status symbol few people had.

I could tell right away that this car belonged to nice people who had good taste.

"Not bad," I thought to myself and began to think maybe my luck had finally changed. It turned out as I got older that I'm not an automobile enthusiast, and to learn that humans had named that *thing* after my most regal and impressive relatives, the jaguars, is a joke! So – as soon as I finished my brief assessment of my surroundings, I went to sleep in my new owner's lap.

When I awoke the car was about to descend into the garage of a huge skyscraper in the heart of Manhattan.

Later on I found out I was at Sutton Place – the most elegant neighborhood in New York City at the time – and in the most desirable building of the moment – 60 Sutton Place South.

I learned as time went by that Manhattan is the birthplace of a lot of trends. Real estate was no exception and the time would come when living in buildings like Trump Tower was a real status symbol. But I'm not much into all those things and for the time being, it was enough for me to know that, for the first time in my short life, I wasn't cold anymore.

Konny carefully parked the car in its spot in the garage; we all got out and went up the stairs that led from the garage to the huge lobby of the apartment building. Fern held me tight as Marcie petted me every now and then, and Cory and Konny followed closely behind us.

If in the car I had begun to suspect that good fortune had smiled on me, I was convinced of it the moment I entered my new home.

The apartment was beautiful! It was warm in there and not at all dark. There was soft, diffused light everywhere, and the place seemed enormous to me. Later I discovered there were only four and a half rooms and two bathrooms, but at that moment just the thought of all those corners to investigate made my head swim with joy. The only sad note was when I realized how much fun I could have had there if my mother, and sister and brother could have shared this with me.

My folks took me right into the kitchen and gave me something to eat and drink. They weren't very well equipped to serve and feed a cat, but at that time my palate wasn't nearly as refined as it is now, so that day everything pleased me.

After feeding me, my owners set me up in the kitchen, closed the door and went to the movies.

I ate a little, looked around, and decided the best thing for me to do for the time being was to get some more sleep.

XI | Learning The Rules

My new owners had decided to let me roam freely around the apartment when they were at home and could keep an eye on me, but to put me in the kitchen during the time when they were out working, and at night when they went to sleep.

They didn't know me very well and they were afraid that my manners might leave something to be desired. They had a lot of nice things in the house and Fern especially – because she was already becoming very attached to me – didn't want to run the risk of having to give me away on Konny's orders because I had ruined or broken something! You see Konny was a "picture straightener". I think today you call it OCD (obsessive compulsive disorder). And he was a Virgo to boot. So when he walked into a room, invariably the first thing he would do was to go over to some picture and straighten it because the housekeeper had moved it a fraction of an inch while dusting. And he was a perfectionist. So nothing was ever good enough.

Anyway Fern was right to be concerned because, in fact, there almost was a disaster on the second day of my stay.

You see I mistook the shag rug under the dining room table for a grassy field. I know some of you reading this now probably don't even know what a shag rug is. You're more into Berber carpeting or bamboo flooring – but this was the '60s and shag rugs were the trend of the day. There was no Martha Stewart to tell us they were tacky to say the least.

Luckily, Konny was out and Fern noticed the mess right away and cleaned it up in a flash. Then she scolded me and showed me once more where she had placed my real toilet – the kitty litter box – in the guest bathroom off the den.

But now, tell me honestly, is it my fault that in those days they insisted on making long pile rugs that looked so much like grass? It's true that the rug wasn't green, but rather a dark blue, but even these days you never can tell what color something is supposed to be. And anyway, it was only my second day in that place – I didn't have my bearings yet. But for her to think I would continue to err in perpetuity really grossly underestimated my sensibilities and the upbringing my mother gave me before she passed away.

So, to continue with my story, in the kitchen of my new home there were two doors. One – the service entrance – led to the building hallway. The other led to the living room. This door did not reach the floor. There was quite a large space left on purpose, according to Konny, to allow the air to circulate.

Fern had understood right away that I was small enough to fit under this door and had shown Konny how she was going to put a rag, or a towel, on the floor – and stuff it into the opening so that I would not see this space between the floor and the door.

But, after a few days of being cooped up in the kitchen while Fern and Konny were at the office, I got bored. I knew every nook and cranny of the kitchen. There was nothing left to discover so when I got to the door, I looked at it, tried to see under it, and extended a tentative paw.

Can you imagine my surprise, and the fascination of the bottom of that door, which instead of being hard like the rest of the wood, was soft at the bottom and pliable? Furthermore, it moved! I flattened myself out on the floor and pushed with both paws.

It was a miracle! Suddenly I could see the living room and I knew right away I could get out. Now when I remember that space – because the rag was removed that very day (and anyway, we moved not long thereafter) – I really don't know how I managed to get through. But I was small for my age – I was about three months old then, and also, I didn't know the "impossible" existed. So, I flattened myself out as much as I could; exhaled to help my endeavor; and shimmied my way through that narrow space.

That evening when my owners came home they found me asleep on one of the living room armchairs which was to become *my* space. They didn't put me in the kitchen anymore.

XII | Being Photographed

A wonderful week passed. One evening, however, I was startled again, because my owner decided to take pictures of me. Without even asking! Konny was a professional photographer, in addition to being a writer, director and OSCAR–winning producer, so maybe I should have been flattered. But I was sound asleep when the flash of his camera shattered my dreams!

And anyway, I don't like to sit still – especially when others want it and not me. I'm against everything people want to impose on me just like that – on principle. I'm independent and an individualist. But

Konny's a good photographer and used to getting his way. So, even though I resigned myself reluctantly to pose a little, they came out quite well, don't you think?

Incidentally, I didn't say or write those captions. Fern interpreted my expressions and that's what she thought I was thinking. Actually, sometimes she came pretty close, I have to admit.

"Did I say you could take my picture?!"

54

"After all, I'm sooooo shy!"

"Are you sure that's the right angle?"

"I really like this dignified pose the best."

"Get that thing away from me!"

*"Are you trying to give me enough rope
to hang myself?"*

"A little glamour never hurts."

"Did you say look seductive or menacing?"

"This modeling business is a great big bore, isn't it?"

"How much longer is this going to take?"

XIII | They're Trying To Kill Me

Things were going along too well – I knew it! About a week after I had arrived in my new home I found myself in that poor excuse for a "jaguar" again. As I told you, I don't like cars (having been hit by one at a very early age) but from that day on, my dislike grew to astonishing proportions.

So, for a while I traveled calmly in Fern's lap. Then the car stopped, she picked me up and took me into a drab, grey building while Konny had to find a parking space on the street.

Fern and I went into a room with a desk in it and a lady dressed in white sitting behind it. To the left I could see another room with a cabinet full of bottles against one wall and a large aluminum table in the middle of the room. I could hear the distant barking of dogs. I didn't like that place one bit!

After a while a man in a white jacket appeared and motioned to us to follow him.

We entered that other room as he closed the door behind us and I suddenly found myself on top of that aluminum table, which incidently was really cold! Then, without any advance warning whatsoever – and no apology – that character stuck a thermometer into me. (And he didn't stick it into my mouth, if you know what I mean.) Naturally, I rebelled. I mean, what kind of thing is that to do? And in public! Besides, I wasn't sick. I hadn't even sneezed!

But they were holding me forcibly on that darn table. And that wasn't the worst of it. As soon as he finished with the thermometer, that guy (my owner called him "doctor") grabbed a handful of my skin and stuck a large needle into it. Well, then I really raised my voice in protest. And to what avail? They gave me another injection!

Then the doctor said, "We'll have to check for worms because the stomach is distended."

"You see," said Fern to Konny who had just come in. "I told you its stomach was too big." (Of course my stomach was too big. From starvation!! I'd like to see somebody who has suffered hunger like I have for almost two months who doesn't have a swollen stomach. Worms? What worms?? Was he kidding?! I don't even like those things!)

But then came the worst part of all. They went away and left me there, those new owners of mine. I knew things had been going too well. It felt like old times again.

I stayed ten long days in that place stuck in a cage surrounded by other animals in cages. Not that they were mean to me, but I almost wished I was back in the chicken coop where at least Marcie and Cory came to talk to me. Here everyone ignored me (except to feed me and take care of my health – I have to be fair) because they were too busy caring for other animals who you could see were mostly a lot sicker than I was.

XIV | Home Again

Well, I had just about resigned myself to my new destiny when one day the assistant came and took me back into the front room.

Lo and behold – who should I see standing in front of me if not Fern! (Her complexion was a little darker – because I found out later – she had been in the sun, but there was no mistaking her sweet face. My heart pounded in my ears).

She took me into her arms, smiling happily, and we went out. We got into a yellow car (it was a "taxi") full of suitcases. Konny was in the car too and even he seemed really glad to see me. I thought I must be dreaming because I was so happy.

It turned out they had been on vacation in the Caribbean and had left me at this place which I found out was not only for sick animals but also for those of us who needed a place to stay while our owners had to go away. It sounded like they'd had a great vacation but as Fern said to Konny – coming back and getting me was the best part of the trip!

Fifteen minutes later I was "home" again. We went up in the elevator, entered the apartment, and I discovered the third room – the den – had become MY room. I guess they had managed to do that before going away. There was a little bed (where I've never slept, because I much prefer to sleep wherever – and whenever – I feel like it).

There were also various toys (a stuffed mouse, rubber balls, and many other playthings), but actually I would rather knock down a pencil or pen from the desk, or chase a piece of paper or a ball of string.

And finally, there were also "my" bowls – for water,

for milk, and for fish or meat. These too I rarely use –
like only late at night when everyone's asleep – because
I prefer not to eat alone. So, I eat in the kitchen just as
soon as my mistress has finished preparing everything
for me. And sometimes, I'll carry tidbits of food into
the dining room so I can eat where my family eats. Why
should I be an exception? Don't you agree?

Anyway, all in all, after I returned from my stay
at the doctor's place, we had a rather peaceful time in
our lives. Well, except for the night when Fern came
home from the office and saw me with a tooth sticking
out of my mouth. She looked at me in horror. (What's
so awful, I asked myself?) She looked once more at
me with the dangling tooth and then whispered: "But it
wasn't like that yesterday."

Her eyes immediately filled with tears which
streamed down her face. (It seemed like a flood to me.)
She carried on like that all evening long until she had
been assured by at least three people, (Cory included),
that kittens lose their baby teeth just like children do.
It's just that we cats lose them when we're about three
or four months old – or however old I might have been.

Poor Fern. Who knows how many disasters she

imagined had happened to me during her absence? Like me, hanging by the mouth someplace and, of course, a tooth had become dislodged. And knowing her by now, she must have imagined many more catastrophes (no pun intended). You see, she's a writer and drama (or should I say melodrama?) comes naturally to her. She had written, shot, edited and visualized my whole catastrophic accident in a matter of seconds and the film kept playing in her head.

Fortunately, by the next day, the tooth was gone (I haven't the vaguest idea where it went) and she forgot the whole thing – and so did I.

XV | Shell Shocked

Oh, I almost forgot to tell you about the time I "invaded" my master's most treasured domain.

Konny was an avid snorkeler. And Fern loved the whole underwater world as well. I guess that's why when they went on vacation it was usually to the beautiful islands of the Caribbean. And apparently, way before he even knew Fern, Konny had always gone to exotic places where he could spend hours floating in the water admiring the fish and incredible coral displays. Sad to say that today that world, too, is changing and withering away – but according to Fern in the '50s and

'60s you could walk right into the water from the beach and see extraordinary fish all around you – angelfish, groupers, spotted morays and her favorite fishes – which have almost disappeared from the seas – the little upright sea horses that hovered an arm's length away.

In those days – when people were less ecologically savvy – you could bring back extraordinary shells and reef coral that are protected species today, and Konny had quite a collection. So, when he moved into this apartment on Sutton Place, he converted a closet at one end of the living room into a walk-in bar which doubled as a display for his trophies. Black velvet covered the back wall, providing a dramatic backdrop for the larger shells and coral which were offset by a gold frame – and the bigger trophies were surrounded by smaller, unique shells of various sizes and colors.

It was an amazing display and I think the smell of the sea lingered in that area and it called to me. So one day when my owners were away, I headed toward that closet-bar to do some exploring. I had a feeling it might really be off limits but it was the last remaining bastion of unexplored territory in the apartment so the temptation was too hard to resist.

That night when Fern came home and the lights

went on, she spied some faint paw prints on the black velvet backdrop and I thought she was going to faint she got so pale. Instead she quickly wiped them away and didn't even have the strength left to chastise me in any way. I don't know how I got paw prints on the velvet. I must have stepped on some dust along the way and then used the back wall to stretch my back, which I usually do at least several times a day.

I actually liked that place a lot and since there hadn't been any major consequences after the paw prints on the velvet, I visited it almost every day. That's how I forgot on a Saturday that my owners were home.

Konny was watching television in the bedroom and Fern was reading in the den. It was very quiet and I wandered around until I got up to the bar, jumped up, stretched out, and apparently fell asleep.

When Fern finished reading and walked into the living room she did a double-take. No, there were no paw prints on the velvet. Worse. There was me, stretched out among the precious shells, using one of them as my pillow.

Fern knew she and I were on very thin ice here. But apparently she was so amazed at how carefully I had draped my body among those treasured trophies, she simply had to share it with Konny. She took a deep breath, steeled herself, and whispered "Konny come and see where Destiny's sleeping."

Konny apparently took one look at me and… no – he did not blow his stack! Like any good photographer, he reached for his camera (which was always close at hand) and the flash again startled me out of a wonderful dream.

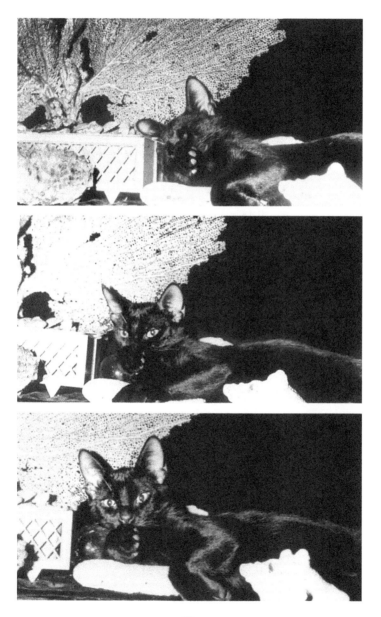

The photo session was over in a flash (no pun intended) and Fern picked me up gingerly so as not to displace any of the shells. Then they scolded me and told me that the bar was not a place for me. It was "off limits!" But it was hard not to go there because there were so many things to see. So I made sure to explore there only when my owners were out. The trouble was I occasionally knocked a shell or two onto the floor. And when Konny came behind the bar to fix himself a drink, sometimes he didn't see the shells on the floor and he accidentally stepped on them.

Now Konny was a pretty big man. Not that he was so tall – just stocky, I guess you would say. Anyway when he stepped on them, the shells were reduced to a million pieces. You could say they then resembled the sand on the beaches they came from. And he got awfully mad when that happened so Fern was always afraid he was going to kill me, or throw me out, but Konny was unpredictable. He could flare up into an uncontrollable rage and then it all went away, as you probably figured out, because I'm still here.

Well, to get back to what I was saying –we lived a relatively peaceful existence for a while until I found myself back in that darn car again!

PART THREE
Weekends In The Hamptons

XVI | I'm A Weekend Commuter!!!

I know, Cinzia, that you people in Italy have only recently begun to commute out of the cities for "weekends". Well, here in America, it's been a mania for years. Especially in places like New York!

Every Friday night everyone hops on a train, or a bus, or gets into a car to travel for let's say two to three hours on average, only to meet up with the same friends they see in the city. Only the location has changed. They have drinks, eat too much food in restaurants filled with the same old familiar faces, and maybe watch a little television or go to see a movie that's playing in the city as well. But I guess they like the change of scenery, so who am I to say – or criticize, that is?

Anyway, by now I know what it means to be a "week–end commuter" only too well, but that day when I found myself back in the Jaguar again, I had no idea I was about to become a weekend commuter of the first order.

As you already know, I don't like to travel. Especially by car. I'm not an automobile enthusiast – unlike Fern who *loves* cars, especially really fast ones. I mean if she could afford a Ferrari, or a Lamborghini, or these days, a McLaren, she would be in seventh heaven. Even today – at her age! Can you imagine?!

I suppose it's because she learned to drive in Rome – when there were no traffic lights! I think that's one of the reasons she's always liked Jay Leno so much. He loves (and understands) cars and cats! Just like Fern. Maybe it's because he's part Italian and she was born in Italy. Who knows?

When people marvel at the Camaro she's driving these days (it's vintage by now – a 1998 – but in great condition!) I've heard her tell friends that her love of sports cars started when she learned to drive in Rome where she lived as a young newlywed – "a hundred years ago" as she is wont to say! In Italy, especially years ago, all the drivers were race car drivers at heart and I guess she caught the bug back then. Of course, that was many years ago and she laughs when she recounts how the Italians drove in those days when there were no traffic lights anywhere in the city! She was there when they put the first one up – on Porta Pinciana, I think she said.

Apparently it was the biggest joke to all her Italian friends – the Formula One driver wannabes. The Italian authorities of course knew and understood this – so after midnight the light changed to a flashing yellow signal because they knew no self–respecting Italian driver would pay attention to a traffic light late at night when there was little or no traffic. Ah well, as she says – those were the good old days!

But that's Fern – not me. So when these weekend trips began I complained loudly several times. Once I even tried to run away. That is, I jumped out of her arms and ran down the hall back to our apartment door. I wanted to make her understand that I really didn't want to go anywhere, especially in that Jaguar. All to no avail. She picked me up again explaining that it was time to go and that she couldn't leave me in the apartment all alone, so I resigned myself to my fate.

I remember that first weekend very well. The trip seemed endless, but since we were traveling at night, I slept most of the way.

After a few hours we arrived in a place where there were many doors – all in a row, which led to some rooms I guessed. I didn't know it at the time but we were at the Driftwood Motel on the beach between Amagansett and Montauk in the Hamptons – an area on the southern tip of Long Island that stretches from Westhampton to Montauk and which today has become the playground of the rich and famous. In the summertime it's now absolutely the trendy place to be!

It turned out we had the largest, corner room at the end of a long walkway. Since it was already late, my owners quickly unloaded the few things they had brought and we all went to sleep on the very large bed. There was a daybed besides the large king-size bed where eventually I would nap during the day time, but at night I much preferred to share the king-size bed and to feel the warmth of their bodies as we all slept.

"We had the corner room at the Driftwood Motel."

At that time I was still very timid and easily frightened. The memories of my past life – the cold, the dark, the hunger – weren't nearly as vague as they are today. So you can bet your bottom dollar that the next morning, when we all got up, I didn't even dream of crossing the threshold. Not on your life!

This cabin wasn't like our home in the city, but it was warm; they were feeding me; and they loved me here too. Go out? What for?? But the decision wasn't left up to me.

Suddenly, the day after our arrival that first weekend, I found myself again in Fern's arms. She held me tight and took me out.

Outside it was very cold. I think it was only April or a very cold early May. Anyway, there was a hateful wind and I could hear a frightening noise which I couldn't define. Later on I learned it was the ocean waves breaking on the shore. I was at the beach!

Maybe, my friends, the thought of being at the beach fills you with joy. But that day, everything filled me with terror. Can you imagine how I felt with that horrible, rhythmic noise which kept getting closer, and the wind howling in my ears?

I began to tremble, more from fright than from the cold, but Fern couldn't tell the difference, so she tucked me inside her jacket and hugged me close to her chest. That was nice but I wasn't reassured and finally she understood that the beach held no particular fascination for me – at least not right then.

She quickly took me back to the room where I thanked Heaven, jumped immediately onto the daybed near the radiator and got ready to take a good, long nap.

XVII | Maybe It's Not So Bad...

The second weekend went a little bit better. First of all, instead of a cold, windy, wintry day – the sun was out and you could feel Spring in the air. Also, they didn't try to take me down to the beach again, and I felt brave enough to venture across the threshold.

Not that I went very far that time, don't get me wrong. I only went a couple of feet or so. Then I rushed back into the room, heaved a long sigh of relief, and felt myself very much akin to those brave explorers of old like Columbus and the rest. After that great exertion I had to sleep for at least three hours in familiar surroundings to restore myself.

That evening, however, as my owners started to go out for an early evening walk – I ran out the door and waited for them.

They looked at me quizzically, and I turned and walked a few steps, hoping they would follow me. Finally, Konny smiled at Fern, and she shrugged and said, "I guess she wants to go with us."

That evening was a great break-through for me. We walked out onto the sand which felt soft and cushy to my unaccustomed paws. As we headed towards the ocean I decided I liked the feel of the sand much better than the wooden floors or rugs back in our place in the city.

As we got closer to the ocean I could see the waves breaking gently on the shore. Now I know it must have been low tide because this time the sound of the surf seemed soothing to me, not menacing, so I wasn't a bit afraid.

I started to run around Konny and Fern, and then ahead of them, and then behind them, all the time enjoying the feel of the sand sifting through my toes and nails. Fern giggled and told Konny I was acting just like a dog, which I'm not sure I appreciated, but still we were having a really good time. The evening was getting darker, and the first stars were just beginning to appear, when Fern scooped me up, declared that was enough for one evening and we headed back to our room at the motel. But not before she made her "wish upon a star" which she always did – as well as touching gold and wishing on the first sliver of the new moon whenever it appeared – just as her mother had done, apparently, ever since Fern was little. I think I heard her explain to someone one day that it was an old Russian custom – or superstition – as the case may be.

By the third weekend, I felt like a "regular" at the beach and decided it was high time to really explore the surroundings. So, on a Saturday afternoon, I took a long walk (very cautiously, of course) through the dune grass.

What a wonderful experience that was! How many things there were to discover! What fun!

Here in Montauk – and probably other places along the coast as well – to keep the sand from eroding, they had planted a special type of "dune" grass. It was fairly high, planted in little bunches every six to eight inches apart, and made a wonderful forest for me. And how much life there was in that forest!

Crickets, grasshoppers, ants, butterflies, and even field mice. It felt like I was living in some wonderful dream and from that day on I could hardly wait to go roaming over the dunes. It was during one of these exploratory excursions that I came to know the rain again.

I say "again" because I knew the rain very well when I was very little. I mean before the accident and even after Marcie found me and put me in the chicken coop, come to think of it.

In fact, to be honest, I can't remember even one nice, sunny day during the first months of my life. It was always snowing, or raining, or hailing during the time I was roaming around, lost in the world. But ever since I had moved to Sutton Place the weather, just like hunger, was no longer a problem in my life.

Anyway, it happened like this. My walks kept getting longer and longer and I was traveling further and further away from the motel. One day, as I was returning home, I felt a drop of rain on my back. Now rain doesn't really hurt us cats because our fur acts as a sort of "raincoat". It's just that we don't particularly like it, so I began to run.

I still had quite a piece to go when it really started to pour. Naturally, I accelerated my pace.

Finally, I spotted my door, so I put on the last burst of speed that every racer saves for the finish line.

Well, I was going too fast. By coincidence just then Fern became really worried because of the heavy rain and decided to go out to look for me. She opened the door just in time to see me fly, or should I say "skid" by – right under her nose. I put on the brakes – so to speak – skidding along on my hind paws and my tushie, to be frank. I'm sure I looked just like those animals in those cartoons that we think are made up just to be funny – but it happens just like that in real life too! Finally I came to a stop, turned around, retraced my steps, hung my head in shame, and crept sheepishly into the room. You can imagine how she laughed! Not only that, she used it as a joke to tell all her friends for weeks.

Now that I can look back on that day with some objectivity – I have to agree it was pretty funny. But at the time – I wasn't laughing.

XVIII | I Know What I Like!

Although my life was really enviable, nothing is perfect in this world. And, just like everybody else, I had my good days and bad ones; my likes and my dislikes.

For example: after those first few times, I enjoyed being at the beach. But, as much as I liked it, getting there was always a problem for me.

By now you've probably understood that there was a kind of "cold war" between me and the Jaguar. First of all, let me say again, I see absolutely no resemblance between my relatives, the magnificent jaguars of the jungle, and that Jaguar with four doors!

When I move (whether I'm going fast or slow) it's always graceful and very quiet. The same goes for my jungle relatives. But that Jaguar on four wheels?! It reminds me of a blender making a milkshake; or of a washing machine when it spins to get all the water out of the clothes and looks like it's doing some kind of African dance.

The worst part is that *I* feel like a milkshake when I ride in it. It must be different for human beings, but I'm very little, and for me every vibration is like an earthquake. Not to mention what it's like when it hits a pothole in the street. And I don't have to tell you how many of those there are in Manhattan!

You know, I really don't get it. That Jaguar has six eyes in front – to see the fog, for distance viewing and for close range things – but the potholes in the streets and highways? It doesn't see them! As for the noises… like the wind that comes in through the open windows and whistles in my ears, or the pressure when we enter a tunnel or go up a hill … well, really, forget it. But I must admit that our "Jaguar" takes us where we want to go and I don't think my relatives, the jaguars, would be nearly as obliging.

Food is another problem in my life. Or maybe it would be more accurate to say in Fern's life.

We had settled into a routine in the city. In the mornings Fern would get up fairly early and serve me breakfast before she got ready to go to work. But on the weekends (before we started going to the beach) she and Konny liked to sleep late.

Well, I can appreciate that they wanted some extra rest but by eight-thirty or nine o'clock in the morning I would be hungry. So I started jumping – very gently, you understand – onto the bed and settling on Fern's chest. Fortunately for me – most mornings when I came in she was sleeping on her back so settling onto her chest with my face close to hers wasn't very difficult.

I'm sure on occasion I could see a smile forming on her lips. But, she didn't say anything, and she didn't open her eyes, so finally one day I figured I needed to give her an additional nudge if I was ever going to get fed. It was on those mornings that I would take my paw (nails tightly drawn in, of course) and lift her eyelid to see if she was awake. If it didn't work the first time, I would try again, until I could feel her stomach going up and down as she tried to suppress her giggles. Well, when that happened I knew breakfast wasn't far behind and I would sit back, look at her eyes, and then jump down, hoping to lead the way as she sleep-walked into the kitchen and got me something to eat.

By now my palate is quite refined and no matter how much I love Fern, I can't change my tastes, compromise my principles, or lower my standards.

The first problem began when my owners brought me back home from my stay at the doctor's house – or "hospital", as it was called. At the time he sold Fern a whole case of the stuff that I hadn't been able to get used to in the ten long days I spent there.

It's true that I ate some while I was there, but I figured they had nothing else, and it was always better than hunger cramps.

But at my house things were different. I knew that because I had eaten very well there before they took me to the doctor's and went away. So, the first time Fern offered me a whole bowl full of that awful stuff, I sniffed at it, and walked away without even touching it.

I did the same thing the second day and Fern began to suspect I didn't like the food recommended by the vet. She looked at the huge case full of cans with that stuff and then called the doctor.

"The cat doesn't like your cat food, doctor," my mistress said to him, putting the phone on speaker as she paced around the kitchen.

"That's all right," he answered, "...it's good for her. Just leave it out. When she gets hungry enough, she'll eat it."

"But doctor, it's been two days since she's eaten. She's hungry now."

"Don't give in," said that so–called friend of mine.

"But the cat will hate me," explained Fern, rightfully so. "Well, better the cat should hate you, than that I should."

And so their conversation ended. But the doctor

didn't know us very well. My owner can be as stubborn as a mule, but not where I'm concerned. And not when she's not convinced of something. This business of forcing me to eat something I didn't like, didn't sit well with her. She remembered that her mother had never forced her to eat anything she didn't like when she was little, and after all, she had grown up o.k. Besides, she had more faith in my natural instincts regarding what was good or bad for me than in the science of men.

I immediately understood all this from the tone of her voice, the expression on her face, and the look in her eyes. So I knew my hunger was about to end.

You can imagine my chagrin when at dinner time I found the same horrible junk in the bowl she put down in front of me. Well, I realized right away that I had to make sure she'd understand that I didn't like this food at all, and I wasn't going to eat it.

So, first I sniffed at it (and made sure Fern was watching me carefully). Then I scratched the floor around the bowl with my paws (the way I do in the box full of litter which serves as my toilet) as if I was trying to cover up the food the way I do after I've peed or pooped in my litter box. Then I walked out of the kitchen with my head held high and an indignant air.

That did it. Fern got the message. She immediately threw that stuff away and then called me back and gave me something really good to eat.

Everything went along fine for a few days. But, you see, I tire quickly of things. So, even if I like something very much, after three days I can't bear to look at it anymore. To this day my owner has to rack her brain to devise new menus for my mealtimes.

For instance, lately I've had a real craving for liver. Especially those little chicken livers. I like them raw or cooked. As for meat – right now I prefer veal. On the other hand, I've completely lost my appetite for fish – and for some time now – I've been trying to find a way to make Fern understand this.

XIX | We're Moving On Up!

Oh yes! With all the explanations about my names: Destiny, Espresso, and Katzchen – I forgot to tell you that when my owner calls me, she almost never uses any of them.

Instead she makes a noise…how can I explain it to you? …Oh…right. It's like a kiss. Yes – go ahead – send a kiss into the air… a couple of them actually. That's it! You've got it. That's how she calls me. She does that two or three times and usually when I hear her, I come running.

She always gets a big laugh when she sees me coming, especially if I'm running at top speed, and she says to Konny, like that day at the beach if you remember, that I'm just like a dog. If it wasn't for all the love I hear in her voice when she says that – I'd get really mad. Imagine?! A dog?!

Speaking of dogs, once a dog came to visit us at the beach. If I hadn't been so scared, I would have laughed in his face. Goodness, he was funny!

I learned later he was a "basset hound", but to me, with those fat legs that were almost shorter than mine, that body that never ended, and a stomach that almost scraped the floor, he looked to me like something from another planet.

As soon as I saw him come in, I jumped out of Fern's arms so quickly that I accidentally scratched her. (She knew I didn't mean to.) Anyway, I hid behind the couch and peeked out from underneath.

Everyone was calling to me and saying that the dog wasn't going to harm me. He only wanted to play, but I didn't believe it. As it is, I don't like to fool around very much so you can imagine how eager I was to play with that dog, who with a friendly slap of his paw could send me flying into outer space. No thanks. Not for me!

The visitors stayed a while and then left and I came out from under the couch, went to sit on the windowsill where the afternoon sun still warmed and calmed me as I settled down to get some sleep.

Anyway, I was telling you about how Fern blows kisses into the air when she wants me to come in after dinner to go to sleep. But first I have to fill you in on our living arrangements at the beach.

We had spent the weekends in late May and early June at the motel. But Konny loved the beach and had always wanted to have a house in the Montauk area for the summer – especially after his motor boat had perished during one of the "Nor'easters". That's a winter storm that often plagues the East Coast during the wintertime. So, on one of our weekend visits, Konny and Fern met with a local real estate broker and in mid–June he showed them a beautiful house high on a hill on the sandy beach overlooking the Atlantic. It had a separate guest house, and a detached garage as well. I didn't go with them but they were very excited when they came back and I could see this meant a lot to them.

"Nice, don't you agree?"

I found out later that another reason Konny wanted to have a house for the summer was because he hoped his daughter, Cory, and her best friend, Marcie, (whose mother, if you remember, had died that year), would come to spend some time with them.

By July 4th Konny and Fern were sufficiently settled into the house to invite all the personnel from Konny's small New York film company (Marathon International) to a beach BBQ in Napeague. That's a place just between Amagansett and Montauk where our beautiful house sat on the dunes overlooking the beach. Cory and Marcie were due to join us as well for the whole summer. I could hardly wait to see them again. To have their company for the whole summer was very exciting for me.

By the time we moved into the house I felt very much at home in the Hamptons and I looked forward to exploring new territories and to having the little girls who had been my saviors, join us.

We all settled easily into our routines. Cory and Marcie had the small guest room with the twin beds and I spent most of my daytime hours sleeping on one of the beds. Their room got a lot of afternoon sun so it was the perfect place to nap.

Konny and Fern had the big master bedroom on the opposite side of the house, and we all enjoyed breakfast together in the large country kitchen overlooking the beach. There was also a living room with a fireplace (not that we needed one, although some evenings it did get pretty cool), an alcove near the kitchen for the dining table and chairs, and a lovely sun porch overlooking the ocean which was my second favorite place to sleep.

After the July 4th holiday BBQ Konny and Fern got into the habit of taking long weekends away from the office – and sometimes one, or the other of them, would stay at the beach for the whole week while the other one came back – usually early on Friday morning and then one of them would leave again for the city on Sunday evening or Monday morning.

Konny had also bought a small used car (a cute turquoise Nash Rambler) so we would have a car to use locally when one of them took the Jaguar back to the city (hooray!). And Fern decided it would be best to get some help for the time when she would be away. So she interviewed and hired, with Konny's consent of course, a German "au pair" (meaning someone who worked mostly for room and board) named Crystel to help with the shopping and cooking and take care of me and the girls when they both were away.

Of course Konny approved. Crystel looked great in a bikini and was even a good mechanic. I remember many a day when I saw her – feet dangling because she wasn't very tall – as she rummaged around under the hood of the Rambler.

Everyone was really surprised that Fern had hired someone so attractive to stay with us – especially since Konny sometimes stayed at the beach while Fern went into the city. But my owner was pretty sure of herself in her relationship with Konny and it wasn't until Karen, coincidentally another German young miss, came into their lives at the office, that Fern began to feel the pangs of jealousy. However, that's a whole other story that we don't have time for right here.

By the middle of July I had a steady routine. I'd sleep most of the day and then play with the girls when they came back from the beach. In the early evenings, I would go outside and play with the creatures (crickets, fireflies, little lizards, whatever) that surfaced after sunset and made everything in the dunes so interesting.

That is, I would come in around seven or eight o'clock for a snack and then I'd go out again until Fern called me to come in to go to sleep. She would do this by standing at the front screen door and blowing three or four kisses into the night air.

One night, however, I came in to eat a little later than usual and because during dinner I got wind of a mouse somewhere in the vicinity, I didn't go out when I finished eating. Instead, I hid myself in a dark corner of the kitchen – ready to pounce in ambush!

A couple of hours passed. The night darkened. A peaceful silence descended on the house and I fell asleep. (After all, it's much easier to dream of catching mice, rather than wasting time and energy chasing them! Especially on a full stomach. It's bad for the digestion.)

Much to my dismay, I was awakened when I heard Fern calling me, so I went, still sort of drowsy, into the living room.

My drowsiness vanished in a flash because I saw that she was standing at the front door blowing kisses into the wind.

How could this be, I asked myself? She wasn't calling me at all – because I was standing right there behind her. Instead, she was at the screen door, peering into the dark night, and calling out with all her might.

I have to tell you, my friends, that I was rather upset at the thought of another cat in the family. Especially a stranger. It didn't please me at all. The least they could have done was warn me... arrange an introduction... something. But anyway, I, too, went to the door and looked out into the night to see who it might be.

No one was coming yet so we both stood there immobile for a couple of minutes – Fern in her nightgown standing at the open door, and me, seated next to her at her feet. We both peered out into the blackness.

No one showed up so finally Fern sighed, looked very worried, turned and that's when she saw me! "Aho?! Ma da dove vieni?" she asked me, in the Roman dialect, with the usual gesture of her hand (which in case you don't remember means: OK stupid, where on earth did you come from?) And this time there was annoyance, not love, in her eyes and the tone of her voice.

I looked at her, somewhat hurt and annoyed myself, as if to say: You mean, you don't even know that I didn't go out again tonight?

But then she started to laugh and we made up. She picked me up, kissed me, and we both went to sleep.

XX | Looking For Love

But I didn't always come when Fern called me to go to sleep. Not that I did it to spite her. I wouldn't do that. It's just that I wasn't always close enough to where I could hear her.

On those nights when I came home later, if I was lucky, Fern heard me meowing under her window and came to open the door. Otherwise, when she didn't hear me, I was forced to spend the whole night outside.

I didn't mind very much though. Usually it was nice out, and hunting is always better at night, especially towards dawn.

But there was something wrong in my life. It was mid-summer already. At night the stars glittered like a million diamonds in a dark velvet sky. When the moon was full it bathed the beach, and the dunes in its light, and reflected on the ocean casting a magnificent glow over everything ...and I was alone.

I mean, as much as I loved my folks, and they loved me – I was beginning to miss the company of other cats.

It's not easy spending all your time with people. Every now and then you need a breather; a change of air. So, every night, my walks became longer and longer.

I figured this way: during the daytime the other cats that must be around probably sleep like I do, or anyway – stick close to home with their families. At night, though, they too must go strolling around the area like I do, so it should be the most ideal time for a happy encounter.

Well, I won't go into how many miles I covered that summer but they were plenty. And I never met anybody at all!

110

Correction. That's not exactly true! Once, (when we were coming to the beach on weekends and still staying at the motel) towards dawn, I did meet a huge, orange striped cat. I think he was ancient. And I was still very young – maybe six months old or so. He must have been at least a great grandfather already.

However, we did have a nice chat. He even gave me a whole lot of advice (the way I see all older people like to do). Among other things, he told me to stay away from those lights that move along the highway at night. He explained that they were the headlights of cars (that's how they refer to what I call the "eyes" of our Jaguar. Gee, I didn't realize they lit up at night!)

He told me that looking at them could momentarily blind us cats and so prevent our getting out of the way of the car. That's how his father died, he explained. And, come to think of it, that's probably what happened to my mother and me, and how I got hurt when I was little. It was night and I think we were crossing the street. And she was mostly all black. No wonder we got hit by a car. The driver probably never even saw us or knew we were there.

He also told me to be careful what cats I took up

with and, above all, never to go looking for them near the houses, or hotels or motels in the neighborhood. He explained it upsets people to hear our voices in the night as we call to each other and make our dates. He said they get mad because it keeps them awake.

Boy! People are funny – and very selfish! While we sleep they shout, sing, fight, slam doors, and watch television. So? Do we ever complain? No, we don't.

My new friend and I talked until dawn and then he walked me home. The sun was just appearing on the horizon as we sat down in front of my door. Everything was still and bathed in a soft, pink light.

Suddenly, we saw the curtains of the front window move and Fern looked out and saw us.

My great grandfather friend took to his heels and was gone in a flash. I, on the other hand, slinked into our room with a shame–faced expression because this was the first time I had come back so late – or rather – so early. Fern was beside herself.

I found out later that my friend came back to look

for me the following night, but we had gone back to the city and the other guests at the motel chased him away. I never saw him again, that nice old cat.

Meanwhile Fern was obsessing because I don't know what she thought had happened between us but she kept telling Konny that I had come in looking like a mess. She knew something had happened between me and that old orange cat!

Honestly! I was barely reaching puberty – and he was way past "mating" age but she kept ranting that under no circumstances did she want any orange striped kittens!

XXI | Lost Among The Dunes

Later on that summer, when we were already in the house, I often stayed out all night. At those times I would come home around eight a.m., have breakfast, and then sleep most of the day. But one night I felt very bad – not only spiritually, but physically as well.

It's sad to be alone, especially when you really want to be with someone. That night I was very discouraged because I couldn't seem to find anyone with whom to meow a few words in my native tongue.

Besides that, I was very weak because I wasn't

eating very much those days because of my bad mood. I think you humans call it a "depression". Whatever you call it, it's not fun. And also, I covered a lot of miles every night.

That's how it happened that one night, towards morning, I just couldn't go on. I got as far as a motel not too far from our house and felt terribly sick, so I hid under a wooden stairway at the entrance to the motel.

I was nauseated. My head was spinning and I had even sprained one of my legs. I was completely dazed and disoriented. I decided to try and sleep a little in the hopes that that would make me feel better.

I think I got to the motel around seven a.m. and slept until about ten a.m. – when someone discovered me and tried to get me to come out – which I wasn't about to do.

I don't trust people very much, so that's why I had intended to wait for dark before trying to get home. But now I had been discovered. I could no longer stay there. On the other hand, leaving meant being caught for certain. I didn't know what to do. So, I burrowed even further under the building. I went as far as I could get.

Luckily, the people finally understood that I didn't want to come out and they went away. But, every time I tried to leave that place to go home, someone else would appear so I decided the only thing to do was to sleep there until it got dark. Especially because my head was still swimming and I wasn't at all sure I'd find the right way. Meanwhile back at my house pandemonium reigned because of my absence. I've heard my folks tell and retell this story a million different ways.

It seems Fern was walking around with a gloomy face, not saying a word. Marcie was also very worried. Christel, our German "au pair" racked her brain, trying to figure out where I could be. Konny wasn't there because he and Cory had gone down to the beach for an early swim, but as soon as they got back, Fern announced dramatically: "Destiny didn't come home today. She's gone!"

"What do you mean, 'she's gone'?" Konny asked. Then, raising his voice, as if the tone of his voice could make me reappear, Konny said:

"Where is she?! Marcie! Christel! Where's the cat?!"

"We don't know," they answered. "She didn't come back this morning."

Everyone was quiet for a while. Then Konny, getting up, said:

"Let's go look for her."

"Sure! Where are you going to look for her? We don't even know what direction she went in when she went out last night. Where are you going to look for her?" said Fern accusingly, as if it was his fault that I was missing! Then she turned and walked nervously out of the house.

Once outside she sat down at the top of the steps to the porch and looked out into the distance.

Our house was situated at the top of one of the dune hills with other, isolated dunes, all around and the ocean at our backs. Towards the horizon in front you could see part of the main highway and some houses in the distance. Today it's a highly populated area but this was the '60s and there was a vast expanse of empty terrain as far as the eye could see. Fern looked to the right and to the left and out past the highway toward the horizon.

Nothing moved anywhere around the house. Everything was still. Weakly she sent two kisses out into the air, the way she used to do to call me. Nothing. No black cat was to be seen scurrying over the dunes. She tried to call me one more time and then her eyes filled with tears.

That's when, through her tears, she saw the vultures! They were flying in a sinister circle over the dunes not far from the house.

Fern's heart stopped while with her mind's eye she could already see what was the prey of those hateful birds: a small, black cat.

But maybe it wasn't dead yet. Maybe it's just lying there, hurt and bleeding, because no one knows it's there, thought Fern desperately. She got up quickly and headed toward those ominous birds.

After a while she arrived at the spot where she thought the birds – who flew away as she approached – had circled.

There was nothing on the dunes. Fern examined the entire area and every now and then observed the tracks left by various animals. Usually they were dog tracks, but every now and then, she found the imprint of small paws and then Fern would follow them. But they went in all directions and after a short distance, disappeared.

She searched some more but found nothing. Then she returned home, very subdued. There, she slowly took one of the bicycles and headed for the main road.

"Where are you going? To look for Destiny?" shouted Marcie from the doorway.

"Yes," answered Fern. "I'm going to see if she's along the highway."

"Wait for me," yelled Marcie. "I'll go with you," and she ran to get the other bike.

So they both headed for the highway together. When they approached the intersection with the main road, they turned to the right and after a few yards spotted a man in front of a house.

"What do you think, Marcie, should we ask him if he's seen a black cat?" asked Fern.

"Oh yes!" answered Marcie and quickly approached the man.

Fern got off her bike and waited. Then she saw Marcie go to the door of the house after talking to the man. A few minutes later she came running back all out of breath. Pointing in the direction of the house where a woman was standing in the doorway, she blurted: "That woman saw a black cat! At one of the motels this morning! It must be Destiny!"

"O.K." said Fern, indicating a motel in the distance. "Let's try that one. It's the closest."

They mounted their bikes again and headed for the motel. They hadn't quite reached the entrance with the stairway (under which I had slept), when Marcie exclaimed:

"I hear a cat meowing. Oh, Fern, honest. I hear a cat!"

Fern tried to calm the little girl because she didn't want her to be too disappointed in case they didn't find their "Destiny" – but she too felt excited.

121

"Marcie, are you sure? I don't hear a thing."

"Yes, yes! I hear a cat meowing," said Marcie, and then, jumping off her bicycle, she shouted:

"Fern! I see a cat! A black cat! It's Destiny. It's really her!"

Fern, who hadn't seen anything yet, commented: "Honey, there are lots of black cats. It may not be her."

But just then she saw me. I had come out from under the stairway and was walking in the grass near the entrance, calling to them.

It was a marvelous reunion. Fern picked me up and Marcie hugged and kissed me. They left their bicycles there and walked all the way home, gently carrying me.

After a short distance I wanted to get down and go the rest of the way on foot, but Fern didn't trust me. She held me very tightly until we got home.

When we entered the living room and the others saw me, it was like a holiday, and so wonderful I still have to smile when I think of it.

In fact, it was so nice that they had to come and get me at that motel another couple of times during the summer. But, by now, they knew just where to find me so they weren't nearly as worried as they had been that first time and the welcome kept getting cooler and cooler until I finally understood this wasn't a game they wanted to continue to play – and it would be better for me to come home in the mornings by myself.

XXII | All Good Things

The summer was winding down. The girls had gone back to their respective homes – Marcie to the Bronx and Cory to Lakeville, Connecticut – to get ready for the new school year. Christel left to return to Germany. Konny was back at Sutton Place. Fern and I had the beach house to ourselves.

Fern was busy packing up boxes and then going to sit – sometimes alone, sometimes with me – on the deserted beach to look out over the ocean and think – about the future, and the past, and to wonder how things were going to be. As mentioned, it was the '60s. A painful

125

decade in all respects. And Fern was hurting. Being of Russian descent didn't help. They're notoriously pessimistic and sad. "Breast-beaters" Fern used to say.

Even as a child she loved the saddest love songs her mother would play on the piano, and sometimes sing. One of her favorites, when she was like three or four years old, was a French song "Il Pleur Sur La Route" (*It's raining on the street*) – a song about lovers parting. Go figure why a little girl would respond to that!

And now, in her late 20's, some of her favorite Italian songs were things like "Se Le Cose Stanno Cosi" (*If That's The Way Things Are*), "Vecchio Frak" (*Old Cutaway)* about an old gentleman – think Maurice Chevalier – walking along the deserted streets of Paris at dawn thinking about his life and his long lost love, and "Grazie Dei Fior" (*Thank You For The Flowers*) – with lyrics like; Mi han fatto male e pure gli ho graditi, Son rose rosse e parlano d'amore – (*They hurt me and yet I treasured them, they are red roses and they speak of love.*)

The song goes on to say that in the midst of all those roses there are many thorns; painful memories of people who once loved each other. They are pages

126

we have closed with the painful declaration: *It's over. Thanks for the flowers, but if our love is ended, why do you want to torture our hearts?*

All songs about lovers parting, unrequited love, unbearable sadness.

It's no wonder that a friend and neighbor of ours on Sutton Place once said Fern's collection of records (in all languages, I might add) should be titled "Songs to Commit Suicide By". Her multi–national collection of songs included "One For The Road" by Frank Sinatra, "Ne Me Quites Pas" from Jacques Brel and later Laine Kazan, "Yesterday" from Charles Aznavour, and, I didn't know it then, but later what would become our theme song: "My Way" from Frank Sinatra as the relationship between Konny and Fern got stormier and stormier.

Apparently, before I came into their lives – Fern and Konny had had a rocky start to their relationship ever since they re–connected in 1961 – discovering they were both single again.

Konny was divorced from his third wife, Jean, and Fern had finally gotten a proxy divorce from her first husband, Stan, before she returned to the states for one of her cousin's weddings in California.

Konny and Fern had first met in Vegas in 1958 when Konny was shooting his OSCAR–winning short documentary "CRASHING THE WATER BARRIER". And, in fact, if you go on the internet today and Google the title you can see the whole 9–minute film. And, if you don't blink – you will see Fern and Stan (her first husband) among the spectators on one of the days Donald Campbell attempted to break the speed boat record of the world.

She and Stan had been on vacation in Las Vegas from Italy where they had been living since 1956. Stan worked as an attorney for the General Accounting Office at the Rome Embassy and Fern studied singing and focused on being the perfect "hostess with the mostest" for her husband, his colleagues and their friends.

I learned from hearing Fern tell the story of how she first met Konny in the lobby of one of the hotel–casinos along the Las Vegas strip.

It seems gambling always made her nervous. The thrill of winning never made up for the pain of losing as far as she was concerned. Stan, on the other hand, liked gambling and felt if he had won back his initial investment, the rest was "house money" and he gambled freely with it. To Fern – once they won – it was their money and she thought they should leave.

It was on one of those occasions – when Stan was doing well at the craps table and Fern was getting more and more antsy that he gently suggested maybe she should take a walk and get some fresh air or something. His tone was kind so she didn't get upset and took him up on his suggestion.

After wandering around the Casino and then outside, she re–entered the hotel and settled onto a large, comfortable couch in the lobby of the Sahara Hotel, I think she said. Or maybe it was The Desert Sands. In any case, back in the mid-'50s there weren't many hotels along the strip and the ones that were there, according to Fern, were all nice, and elegant.

So, as Fern would tell it, not long after she sat down, these two men carrying clip boards, and camera cases came into the lobby and one of them plopped down at the far end of the couch where she was sitting.

It turned out to be Ken Baldwin, Konny's VP of

production for Marathon International, and Konny, who was producing and directing the documentary. They were engrossed in discussing equipment, schedules, and strategies for their shoot – and Fern, aspiring singer and actress that she thought she was in those days, began to flirt with the man standing in front of Ken. That turned out to be Konny, who, of course, noticed her interest.

The moment he responded by introducing himself and Ken, Fern panicked and immediately said she was waiting for her husband, which didn't deter Konny one bit. He soon invited her – and her husband, he added – to join him the next morning for a car ride to, and then a boat ride, on Lake Mead, where preparations were being made for the first day of shooting. Fern, who loved fast motor boats almost as much as she later came to love fast cars, accepted and she and her husband had a great couple of days with Konny and the crew as history was made. Donald Campbell, after several tries in other places – broke the speedboat record of the world on Lake Mead, and Konstantin Kalser won the first OSCAR ever given to a *sponsored* (Mobil Oil) short film.

After that trip to Las Vegas Fern and Stan had remained friends with Konny, who lived in New York, via long-distance from their home in Rome, mostly via "snail mail" as you would call it today. That was the late '50s and even long–distance phone calls were considered an extravagance and used mostly for emergencies.

It was during this time that Konny's mother – Irmgard von Cube, who was an award–winning screen writer – was instrumental in getting Fern her first role in a feature film.

It was a Mario Lanza picture titled in English "THE SEVEN HILLS OF ROME" but in Italian it took the title of a song featured in the film "Arrivederci Roma" by Renato Rascel, who was also in the picture. It turned out to be one of the last films Mario Lanza would make before passing away in 1959.

Irmgard, as screenwriter on the project, prevailed upon the producers to hire Fern as an extra. Then – thanks to the many rewrites during shooting, Fern's one-day gig as an extra turned into a 3-day job with a couple of lines! What could be better!?

Anyway – that was just one event and a good one but before my time with them – in the long and often turbulent relationship between Konny and Fern which eventually led to marriage and divorce.

She's going to write about it in her autobiography titled "MY ACCIDENTAL LIFE" which she's working on these days – but back when I was living with them I didn't realize that all the "Sturm and Drang" would eventually change my life the way it did!

You see, Konny was a manic–depressive (you now call it "bi–polar") long before Lithium was discovered, and Fern had a lot of baggage of her own. After they reconnected back in 1961 and discovered they were both divorced, Fern was determined not to make the same mistake she had made with Stan. She was going to live with Konny before marriage to see how that worked out. What amazed me after I got to know both of them a little better was the fact that it clearly was NOT working out. Yet – they couldn't stay away from each other. Konny was the oppressor and Fern was the perfect victim. As I've said – I'm often stymied by the things that humans do – and did.

Apparently, before I showed up on the scene, their life was a roller–coaster ride, with her moving in and out of his place, getting apartments of her own, multiple reconciliations and new separations.

I didn't know much about all these things because I was new on the scene but I was beginning to hear stories, and I was witnessing scenes and learning a lot about my "adopted mother's" moods, her hopes, fears and dreams.

I was also beginning to realize that human relations are far more complex than those between us cats. We either like each other or we don't. Humans like each other one day and are ready to kill each other the next day. Things like that always surprised me but I was also beginning to see a lot of other things came into play and colored the interactions between these two people I had come to love and care about deeply.

One of the things that seemed to be troubling Fern greatly was the fact that she was beginning to realize she could not "fix" this relationship. She was in the wrong place, at the wrong time. There was too much work she had to do on herself first and it was unclear if Konny was even willing to do any work from his end.

One of the poems she wrote that summer which she read aloud when she was writing it – mirrored her her guilt, her sorrow and her certainty – knowing that she had to leave.

THE VERY LAST DAWN

The sky darkened that morning,
As it always does before dawn,
But that day it was saying: "I'm sorry –
For by sundown, she'll be gone."

The sky darkened that morning,
Like a day before a storm,
But then it began to brighten,
By the rising sun made warm.

A bird flew up from the meadow,
And headed for the sun,
Chirping its urgent message:
By sundown – she'll be gone."

A cloud rushed to the rescue
And blotted out the sun,
And hissed: "Don't you know," in a whisper
"That by sundown – she'll be gone?"
A breeze came by laughing merrily,
"How silly you all are!
Why by sundown, she'll be laughing,
From someplace, from afar."

He pushed and pulled and pleaded
And cajoled the little cloud,
"It's not the rainy season,
The world can't wear a shroud.
It's just two lovers parting,
It happens every day,
You can't block out the sun for that.
You've got to go away!"

The cloud stood its ground firmly,
And glowered at the breeze,
"My friend, you cannot move me.
I'll stay here if I please."

By then huge tears had gathered,
And soon began to fall,
For the little cloud knew sadly
That she couldn't help at all.

The day was growing older
And the sun was shining down,
But the little bird was silent,
And the little cloud was glum.

The day began to darken,
And night rushed on the scene,
It looked around in panic
And wished it "could have been".

The whole world seemed in mourning
As night spread a gentle shroud,
For it knew beyond a question
That at sundown, she had gone.

Only that had been wishful thinking on Fern's part. She didn't leave. They rented the beach house instead and she was able to play mother to two little girls who, only many, many years later were able to tell her how much that summer had meant to them. Marcie especially – who had lost her mother and was terribly sad, told Fern how much sharing the summer with her had meant. And Cory, who needed the buffer between her and her dad, told Fern for the first time how frightened she had been of visiting because of Konny's volatility and temper. She said she would always ask her mother if Fern was going to be there when she was supposed to come to New York for the weekend.

The funny thing was that Fern had never realized how important she had been to those two little girls. She was so wrapped up in her pain, and her guilt, and me – that she simply did what she believed she needed to do. And looking back all those years later she wished she had been more present and in the moment.

Frankly, I had no idea our lives would go through

so many ups and downs – and how much I would be a part of all those traumatic events. Right now, I knew I was sitting with the most important person in the world to me, looking out at the ocean, from a place we might never be again. Not here. Not ever. Konny was coming from the city with the Marathon van in the morning to take us back to Sutton Place and I was remembering another move – many months before when I had been with my mother and my siblings and how I had never seen any of them again.

Yes, saying goodbye to the beach and the summer was hard for both of us. On the last day as we sat on a rock, looking out at the sea, Fern wrote this poem. I think it captures how we were both beginning to feel.

THE LONELY BEACH

To dream, and to grow old,
And to have the winter of life
Embrace you in its coldness.

The years and dreams have disappeared
Like the children from the Autumn beaches.
The crashing waves echo youth's exuberance
And the wind reminds us of life's fleeting moments –
Too swift to hold, too strong to be ignored.
Oh how I long to bring back the Summer,

With the warmth of its summer sun,
Or recapture the Spring,
With its promise of things to come.

Yet Autumn is here and with it the cold,
Lonely, desolate days.
Yes. Autumn is here.
And Winter will come.

I wondered what the future held for us. But one thing I knew. No matter what, Fern would keep me by her side. I didn't need to be afraid.

By the next day we were both feeling better. The boxes stood ready, Konny showed up with some exciting news about my future – which you will be reading about in my next book, "DESTINY'S CHILDREN" and Fern was looking forward to returning to the city.

And so, dear readers, I've come to the end of this part of my story. There are many other things I have to tell you... like what I thought of television... what I was learning about human relations and how fragile and complicated they can be... but above all, my encounter with Dimitri – that incredibly wonderful Siamese cat who became my mate and the father of my children! But I don't want to tire you. That story is for another time. Right now I'm back at Sutton Place with my owners, but by Christmas who knows where we'll be.

With my folks, you never can tell. I wouldn't even be surprised if one day I found myself in Italy for a nice holiday, and maybe to meet Cinzia – who's a grown lady by now. Anyway, good–bye for now, my friends. And ... arrivederci presto.

Your friend,

P.S. Keep reading. There's a "sneak peek" of my next book in this series starting on the next page!

Sneak Peek!

"DESTINY'S CHILDREN"

I hope you will like this little taste of my new book. And, if you do, please let us know at: theycallmedestiny@ gmail.com

You can also reserve your advance autographed copy of this new book by sending us your name, snail mail address and phone number.

Chapter One

I was pregnant. Oh, please, don't be alarmed. It wasn't an accident. We wanted it – and made it happen. At least, Fern wanted it. I wasn't so sure myself – but it is nature's way so I accepted it and Dimitri had been wonderful.

As mentioned earlier in my story, I had been going out every night at the beach when I got older hoping to find a partner, a companion, someone of my own kind to pal around with. As you also know – I didn't have much success. There weren't many cats rambling around the Montauk dunes in those days –

and probably not now either.

Also, Fern had determined that I should experience the miracle of motherhood before they had me spayed to keep down the unwanted cat population which was growing at an alarming rate.

So, since it became clear that I wasn't having any luck finding new friends – except for that one encounter with that great old cat, Fern decided I needed a little help. She became my matchmaker!

First she contacted breeders who clearly were not interested in mating their prize–winning, pedigreed felines, with a cat of questionable background and certainly with no papers of any kind.

Fern, of course, was convinced I was "royalty" and they would be lucky to have me. Trying to figure out my noble origin, she scoured photographs of cats in every book she could put her hands on and finally decided I had to be at least part Burmese – perhaps with some Siamese mixed in. But the breeders didn't care.

Finally, sometime in August, she located a

breeder who agreed to let us come to see if we could find a suitable mate for me in the hopes I would have a litter.

This breeder lived in an old craftsman-like house in South Hampton with a house-full of cats. She took us up to the attic, or maybe it was just the second floor, but it was pretty open and unfurnished so who knows what it could have been.

There – roaming around the middle of the bare wooden floor – was a huge old Siamese cat. He looked at us warily and as soon as they put me on the floor his back went up, his hair stood on end and he hissed before leaping behind a wooden crate. Fern immediately swept me into her arms and beat a quick retreat, explaining to the breeder apparently this wasn't meant to be. The woman assured my mistress the two cats just needed to get acquainted, but Fern was already out the door.

Back in the car she explained to Konny, who had been waiting for us outside, that there was no way she was going to leave me in there with that vicious old cat for three days. So we went back home and I continued my lonely, nocturnal searches for a mate.

Fern had almost given up hope when, on our last weekend at the beach, Konny mentioned he had found a breeder who sounded very nice and was located about half way home to Manhattan. Her name was Dorothy Shreve and she turned out to be everything – and more – that Konny had said she would be.

She greeted us warmly at the door and welcomed us into her cozy home. After we all got acquainted, Dorothy excused herself and came back with a slender, beautiful, sweet Siamese who looked to be about my age.

We looked at each other and Dorothy and Fern placed each of us on the floor, giving us plenty of space. Dimitri looked me over and turned his attention to Fern. Deciding he liked her, he curled around her legs as she reached down to pet him. Good move, I thought, moving closer to Dorothy so she could get to know me as well. It never hurts to play up to the in-laws. Dimitri and I circled each other, and sniffed, as Dorothy commented she thought we would get along just fine. Fern and Konny agreed.

It was settled. I would stay there for a few days and Dorothy was convinced Dimitri and I would mate. She underscored her concern about finding homes for the future kittens-to-be, and Fern assured her they would be well taken care of and placed with only the best, and most loving families. Nothing except the best would be right for the babies of D and D (Dimitri and Destiny, that is). Fern picked me up and gave me a tight hug and kissed my head. She patted Dimitri, and the new phase of my life was about to begin.

Chapter Two

I really never thought much about it or communicated anything about this until today, but I actually had a very nice three days. Dorothy was very thoughtful and made sure we were well-fed and Dimitri was sweet and gentle. I could easily have spent my life with him but I missed my owners terribly. Even Konny, who complained and criticized a lot, but had a really good heart and I knew he loved me dearly. So when they showed up on the fourth day of my stay with the Shreves, I was thrilled and really ready to go home.

Dorothy told them she was quite sure we had

mated several times and felt certain I would be visibly pregnant within a very short time. By then I don't think Fern really cared anymore. This had been a stressful part of the summer for her and she was just glad to cuddle me and take me home.

It was Cory, the future would-be veterinarian, on one of her weekend visits – who declared I was pregnant. After all, she lived in the country, surrounded by animals of all kinds, so it didn't take her long to see the changes in me.

Konny was proud that his little girl was so intelligent and perceptive but, much to my surprise, Fern had a mixed reaction. She was happy because she was the one who wanted kittens, not me, but now there was something new to worry about: my pregnancy, my health, my giving birth. So many new things to deal with. It would have been better if Cory lived with us but she didn't. She came for the occasional weekend and my pregnancy was going to be a 24 hour, 7 day-a-week ordeal for the next couple of weeks, maybe months. Fern blanched visibly and I could see how nervous she was, but she took a deep breath, picked me up and held me and I could just hope she would be OK.

I wished I could have reassured her that every–thing was going to be all right, but our communications were limited to looks of love, purring, hugs and petting. So, as usual with my owner, whenever she's in a stressful situation, she turns to books and soon into the house came every book imaginable that contained information on cat pregnancies, deliveries, and any bit of advice Fern thought she should have.

Actually, it was good that she had done this because she and Konny learned a great deal about cats and breeding, and whatever they missed, or didn't know, Cory filled them in.

One of the very first books Fern read described the appropriate places where a cat might want to give birth. I knew this because suddenly a bottom shelf in the built–in bookcase in the den was emptied and towels lined the floors making a very comfortable, albeit makeshift and temporary, bed.

A large, brown carton also appeared in the shower stall of the guest bathroom near the kitty litter box. At the bottom of this box was an entire edition of the Sunday New York Times. I studied it for a while and then one night decided it might be an OK place to give birth so I shredded the entire newspaper to make a proper nest. I somehow knew instinctively to do this. It must have been wisdom passed on through the ages. Or at least since the days when the New York Times came to be.

The next morning Fern was amazed. She said to Konny: "It's remarkable. It's as if I'm reading the books in the daytime and Destiny's reading them at night. She's doing exactly what they say."

Well, hardly. I didn't want to disillusion Fern, but it happened the other way around. Some writer must have had a cat who decided a newspaper might make good bedding and, shredding it, made a birthing nest. The writer, admiring his cat's handiwork, must have decided to pass along the information when his cat used that area to give birth to her kittens. So you see, it's not that we cats are reading and learning these things from a book. The books – the writers, that is, are learning it from watching the way we behave. Anyway, when my time came, I decided the bottom of the book case would be the most practical place to be.

As luck would have it, Fern was at Columbia University taking a class that evening, but I couldn't wait. So there I was, alone with Konny, as the kittens started to make their way into our lives.

The first one was born fairly easily, and so was the next one....and the next one... and the next one. Konny and I started to get a little nervous, he more than I, but the kittens kept coming. We were now at six! I was exhausted, and not feeling so well at this point because I knew there was another kitten and this one wasn't coming out so easily.

Konny, who had really been a rock until then, started to get really scared and did the only thing he could think of. He called Cory! She immediately took charge as my seventh kitten started to make its way into the world.

First she told Konny to relax. "Destiny will know exactly what to do," she said. When the kitten was finally out, however, I was too exhausted to lick off the bag. Konny instinctively knew this could jeopardize the kitten's life and told Cory what was going on.

She again told him to relax and suggested he get a pencil with a clean eraser tip that could help open the bag allowing the kitten to breathe. While he did that I was able to rest and catch my breath and after a few minutes as he had succeeded, I was able to take over and lick away the rest of the afterbirth, letting the little kitten breathe. It was November 7th of 1963 and I had just given birth to 7 healthy kittens. Not bad.

Chapter Three

Fern came home to a houseful! Needless to say she was devastated to have missed the births, but enthralled by the tiny creatures surrounding me in the home-made bed.

There were 5 jet black kittens of undetermined sex, 1 black one with white spots and markings and 1 calico – perhaps the only girl in the entire litter. I wasn't even sure about that, but Fern had read in one of her books that all Calico cats are female so who am I to argue until I can make sure for myself.

155

It had been a pretty eventful evening – at least for Konny and me and the little ones, so we all went to sleep early. I was sure now that the pregnancy had gone well, and the births had been brilliant and basically uneventful so now we could all relax and enjoy life, but it was not to be.

Fern moved on to the next tier of books in her "cat-book" library, and now she had new things to worry about. She learned that 7 kittens is an unusually large litter. She knew that the last kitten had been distressed and was sort of the runt of the litter. She read somewhere – who knows where! – that sometimes a mother cat will eat her young, especially if there are any runts in the litter who might not survive anyway. She assumed logically – and from watching – that it wasn't going to be easy for me to feed seven hungry little cats. And, in the middle of all this Konny decided he could no longer live with the baseboards of our apartment/ home as is and that they needed to be painted.

Fern was too preoccupied with her classes, helping Konny in the office, and reading and worrying about me and my brood, so she didn't even challenge or argue with him about his questionable decision to remodel, or rather "repaint", parts of the apartment at this particular moment.

I certainly thought it was rather insane, not to mention insensitive. Painting right now would result invariably in a lot of stress for all of us. And what about the fumes!? They couldn't be healthy for any of us – certainly not my little ones! But logic and other people's feelings were never uppermost in Konny's thoughts when he wanted to do something. It was part of his manic/depressive personality. So the next thing we knew – most of the furniture in the apartment had been moved to the center of each room wherever possible; tarps were spread over everything and life became chaotic to say the least.

Men in overalls appeared every day early in the morning – probably around 8 a.m. and left faithfully at 4 p.m. "Union regulations," I heard Konny say. And Fern wasn't there all the time when the painters were there. She had errands to run, food to buy for all of us, and let's face it – it's not like painting baseboards requires any particular expertise. The most important thing is not to get the baseboard paint on the rest of the walls, especially because the walls in our apartment weren't painted. They were grass cloth on some and vinyl on others so if they weren't careful – there would be hell to pay. Anyway – I think they were really there less than a week, but it seemed like an eternity. And now that I think of it, maybe that's why my "youngest" – the runt of the littler – was always terrified whenever a stranger came to call. He was traumatized by those chaotic few days.

Anyway, one day Fern came back from the office early in the afternoon just after the painters had gone for the day. The first thing she always did when she came home was to come by and greet us, pet us, and love us. That day she came into the den, took one look at us and I thought she was going to faint!

Her eyes widened with terror, she looked all around the room and rushed into the living room of the apartment. I wasn't quite sure what had frightened her so badly – and since I had no way of asking her – I tried hard to relive the moment when she came in so I could figure out what was wrong and maybe try to fix it.

I left the den, walked through the living room and found her in the bedroom looking under the bed. I couldn't imagine what she had lost and followed her into the kitchen. She looked in the bottom cabinets, proceeded into the dining area and collapsed into a chair. She looked at me accusingly and I thought she was about to burst into tears.

That's when I realized what was the matter. When she came home, she had come in to say hello and had counted the kittens. And there were only five in the den with me. Had Konny come in at that very moment I realized what she would have said: "She ate two of her kittens!"

If cats could laugh, I would have burst into hysterics. Honestly. Did she really think mother cats did those things? I've heard of male lions eating their cubs sometimes but come on, we're domesticated. And smaller. And I'm not even sure we'd like how they taste. I gave her my "I can't believe you thought that" look and sidled over to the stack of furniture piled up in the center of the living room. Then I disappeared under the tarp.

Fern followed me after a moment and lifted the cover so she could see. And there I was, stretched out comfortably and beginning to feed the two missing little cats. Fern was so relieved to see us she didn't even focus on the fact that my body, covered with jet black hair, was sprawled out on the snow white couch, feeding two little kittens. If Konny came home to find black hair and milky spots on his coveted white couch it was infinitely more possible that he would kill all of us rather than that I would have eaten any of my kittens.

When he did come home and Fern regaled him with her panic and relief at finding the litter intact, even he had to smile. And fortunately, the couch suffered no damage when Fern carefully took the kittens back to their bed. She explained to Konny, who had figured it out as well, that it was too hard to feed seven kittens at the same time so I had separated them. The problem was with all the furniture stacked up the way it was – the couch under the tarp seemed to be the safest place they could be. The next day I found a better location in the den that was closer and easier to get to and we all heaved a sigh of relief.

Also I heard them say the painters would be leaving in another day. Now perhaps life could resume some semblance of a regular routine, but again it was not to be.

Chapter Four

There's a Russian proverb that goes something like "God forbid it should get any better". I heard Barishnikov, the famous ballet dancer, explain that once in an interview, I think to Barbara Walters. Fern and I had been watching TV and when he said it in Russian, Fern explained it to me. You see, both her parents were Russian and her mother had started teaching her that language when they came to America and she was five years old. Her mom used a book of Russian fairy tales which Fern has to this day. It was written by Alexander Pushkin, a famous Russian writer. Fern's mother thought her daughter was actually learning to read the language but in reality Fern was memorizing all the stories while tracing the lines in the book with her finger as if she was really reading.

Anyway, she explained to me that her mother had told her that expression as well. I guess between wars, revolutions and pogroms, you develop a philosophy that some might consider pessimistic. Thank goodness she tempered that with a happy nature and a moderate sense of humor as well, but I was beginning to understand some of her darker, more tortured moods.

Anyway, in this case, it wasn't going to be an exaggeration. It was 1963 – the beginning of a decade of uprisings, revolts, assassinations and incredible sadness and pain. On November 22nd, when my brood was barely two weeks old, and the painters were packing up to leave, Fern rushed into the house, sank into a chair, turned on the TV and declared to the departing workmen, "President Kennedy has been shot. He's dead".

Over the next three days the grief in the house became palpable. The TV was on non–stop, and on the Sunday when Konny suggested they turn it off to get a little bit of respite from the mourning, Konny's friend, Bronnie Nelkin, arrived and declared that Lee Harvey Oswald, the president's assassin, had also been shot dead. Right on TV. It all seemed unimaginable and surreal.

"Camelot" was over before even getting a chance to fulfill any of its promise. And it would only be the beginning of the violence, not the end of it. There would be Martin Luther King, and Robert Kennedy. Fern wondered how Rose Kennedy could survive; how could she deal with all that sorrow, and the pain, having lost three sons in her lifetime. After Robert Kennedy's assassination, as New Yorkers filed past the coffin lying in State at St. Patricks Cathedral, Fern wrote this poem in a cab as it traveled down Fifth Avenue. I heard it that night when she read it out loud to Konny, whose eyes filled with tears.

FOR THE SPAN OF A MOMENT

> The lines were long
> > in the noon day sun,
> The throng was quiet,
> > just somewhere a song.
> Bobby was dead,
> > the third to go,
> The crowd surged forward

and whispered low.
No violence now –
all was at peace.
The sickness around us,
for a time would cease.
Till the coffin was buried,
the soul laid to rest,
Each man and woman
appeared at their best.
Hearts full of compassion,
eyes filled with tears,
How long would it last?
For how many years?
Till the coffin is buried,
and the soul laid to rest.
For the span of a moment,
we all passed the test.

Now the coffin is buried,
and hate rears its head.
The soul is resting,
and the spirit is dead.
For the span of a moment,
we all united.
For the span of a moment,
one life was cited,
Honored and mourned,

revered and respected,
Its proclaimed dreams
    for a time not neglected.
For the span of a moment
    the dreams of a life
Were held to be just –
    valid – and right.
Till the coffin was buried,
    and the soul laid to rest –
Then the dream was abandoned,
    and the promise was jest.

In memory of Robert F. Kennedy

You can see Fern's Russian soul imbedded in those words and thoughts but today, in retrospect, tell me, was she really that wrong?

Anyway – no matter how bad things can get in the world, a person's (and a cat's) life always interferes. After the painters left, and the TV coverage of the funeral was over, things got back to as normal as they could be, and I had to turn my attention to my brood. Fern did the same.

She was really enjoying the growth of the kittens and laughed when she saw one of them scampering across the living room to disappear into the guest bathroom and scramble into the kitty litter box. She marveled at how they had learned to do that so quickly. Easy for her to say!

Didn't she get that it was my job to teach them? She hadn't shown them the litter box. From the day they were born I had carried each one over to it, made sure they knew where it was, what it was for, and how to get into it. Of course, once we cats know the location of our intended W.C. the rest is basically inbred in us. Unless we're not feeling well, I mean really sick, most felines are happy to be as neat as we can be.

One thing that concerned me though, and Fern as well, was how sickly the last kitten to be born was turning out to be. His nose ran continually, he sneezed all the time, and was often racked with a cat's version of a cough that was heartbreaking.

Between worrying about the runt of the litter, Fern was very busy finding homes for the other kittens. Konny got involved as well. You may think that this process might have caused me a lot of grief, but I think all cats are really prepared to see their offspring leave the nest, or fly the coop, or however you want to put it.

You see our job is to feed them, wean them, and hone the survival instincts they're basically born with. It was one of these sessions that traumatized Fern yet again.

Chapter Five

I, and the kittens, used to wake up quite early. Most days it was around 6 a.m. Konny and Fern, on the other hand, never got up before 7 a.m. Well, on this particular morning, as Fern would tell anybody who would listen, she was awakened by the most terrifying howl coming from the living room. She bolted from the bed, convinced of course, once again, that I was eating my children. She lurched into the living room, with Konny slowly bringing up the rear. They were confronted by a sight Fern tells everyone she will never forget.

I was at the end of the living room closer to the bedroom so all they saw of me was a cat with its hair standing on end, its back up much like the drawings and cartoons of Halloween cats, hissing as loudly as I could.

At the far end of the living room there were seven little "hills" (my kittens) with their hair standing on end, their backs up as fiercely and as high as they could get them, hissing back at me with all their might. Fern was mesmerized, while Konny sleepily declared "She's teaching them" and turned around slowly and went back to bed.

I must say I was really proud of my brood that morning. Because, you see, I realized that even the runt of the litter had great instincts and it wouldn't be hard for me to prepare them for whatever life might bring them. I hoped my owners recognized this as well. I hadn't meant to wake them but I was glad they had witnessed this short lesson, but I wasn't sure how Fern was taking it because she seemed transfixed for a few minutes before she turned quietly and went slowly back to bed.

On a calmer, but equally important, evening

Fern was sitting on the floor surrounded by my brood. She had a small bottle filled with milk that was probably a doll's bottle – and was trying to wean my kittens to drink milk from a bottle as a first step before feeding them some real food. You see, until they were weaned and eating regular food, they could not be given away. Anyway, that night I'm not sure how much milk the kittens actually ingested but I do know there was milk all over everything. On Fern, her robe, the towels she had spread out and a little even on the carpet. I watched, slightly amused, but also grateful because the kittens seemed very contented as they all fell asleep piled helter skelter in her lap and around her feet. And she was happy too. I could tell by the way she was smiling, and petting them gently. It was nice to see her spend a few quiet moments at peace.

One of the things she and Konny had started talking about was names for the seven baby cats. Suddenly, one of the kittens opened his eyes and looked seriously up at Fern with his lovely blue eyes in his round little face. "Oh my goodness," Fern blurted out loud. "You look just like Konny – with his round face and blue eyes. You're 'Konny Kat'. That will be your name".

I'm not sure how Konny felt about having a namesake among my litter and it turned out to be quite funny when several months later Konny Kat went to live with Ken Baldwin, Konny's Exec VP at Marathon International, because, you see, Konny was a perfectionist. He ran a tight and stressful ship. Fern used to say that they took people who worked at 60–75% percent efficiency and reduced them to 10 or 20% by the time Marathon was finished with them. I also heard them say they were the second toughest company in New York to work for – right after Candid Camera which was supposed to be the worst in the city. Anyway, on the weekends Ken would always get shook up when he heard his kids yelling "Here comes Konny" and Ken would think it was his boss coming when, in fact, it was just the little cat they had adopted.

Anyway, the other kittens were beginning to find homes and Fern had determined Konny Kat would stay with us. After all, how could she "give away" a cat called "Konny"? So soon there were just three of us left. Me, Konny Kat, and the still nameless runt of the litter because, of course, they could not give away a sickly kitten.

Then, one day Fern was seated at the dining room table, typing her script on the small portable typewriter she'd had for ages. I was resting on one of the blue armchairs – which was one of my favorite places to be. Konny Kat was probably in the bedroom annoying his namesake, and the little runt was sound asleep on Fern's shoulder.

When Konny (my owner, not the cat) came in and suggested it might be time to think about dinner, Fern agreed, and then she said: "You know, this kitty (indicating the ball of fur curled up on her shoulder) is really too sickly to ever be given away. We might as well keep him." Konny agreed.

I thought my "runt" kitten had been sound asleep, but apparently he must have heard Fern, because I never heard him sneeze again. No runny nose, no cough, no nothing. So, as the saying goes, he may have been sickly, but he wasn't stupid.

And not too long afterwards, Fern exclaimed, "We'll call him D'Artagnan" because he, Konny Kat and Destiny are like the 3 Musketeers!" So now all of us had names, homes, and people who loved us. We were all having a good day.

But as we all know, life doesn't work that way. Good days turn into bad and our lives were about to change dramatically... STAY TUNED.

Bye for now.
See you soon in "Destiny's Children"

Fern and *Destiny*

Additional Books
by Fern Field Brooks

Available now:

"Letters To My Husband…"

"Food… for Thought" with Thom Racina

Coming soon:

"Producers Don't Cry" – from Maude to Monk and everything in between – a memoir

"My Accidental Life" – an autobiography

"More Letters…" – sequel to "Letters To My Husband… - 20 years later!"

"To Heal The Heart – for those of us who have loved and lost and lived to love again.

"We Met By Chance" – a collection of short stories

"I Want To Watch Sunsets" – Poems of Life and Love

Books 2 Cherish

2554 Lincoln Blvd, # 619
Venice, Ca. 90291
310 823–2460